Working with Young People in Secure Accommodation

Locking up young people in secure units is a contentious issue which attracts a great deal of public attention and interest, and a broad range of views. *Working with Young People in Secure Accommodation: From Chaos to Culture* examines the function of these units and offers a balanced insight into the challenges presented to society by young offenders.

Working with Young People in Secure Accommodation explores the work of staff in all types of secure unit with young people. The relationships formed in this setting are key for determining to what extent staff achieve their objective of reducing offending by young people. Using extensive case studies, this book covers:

- The underlying problems of each offender

- How staff can identify and deal with potential problems as early as possible

- Professional issues for management and staff

- Practical suggestions for simple reforms which could dramatically reduce the rate of re-offending

Working with Young People in Secure Accommodation will be invaluable for managers of secure units and practitioners, as it is written from a background of understanding about the real pressure they face day to day. It will also be of interest to other professionals working with young people in the field of youth justice.

Jim Rose is Director of Medway Secure Training Centre in Kent. From 1998 to 2001 he worked as a Professional Advisor to the UK government on the management of young offenders within the prison service.

Working with Young People in Secure Accommodation

From chaos to culture

Jim Rose

Brunner-Routledge
Taylor & Francis Group

HOVE AND NEW YORK

First published 2002 by Brunner-Routledge
27 Church Road, Hove, East Sussex BN3 2FA

Simultaneously published in the USA and Canada
by Brunner-Routledge
29 West 35th Street, New York, NY 10001

Brunner-Routledge is an imprint of the Taylor & Francis Group

© 2002 Jim Rose

Typeset in Times by Regent Typesetting, London
Printed and bound in Great Britain by T J International, Padstow,
Cornwall
Paperback cover design and image by Anú Design

British Library Cataloguing in Publication Data
A catalogue record for this book is available from the British
Library

Library of Congress Cataloguing in Publication Data
A catalogue record for this book has been requested

ISBN 1-58391-199-5 (hbk)
ISBN 1-58391-200-2 (pbk)

Contents

Foreword

Jim Rose uses all his vast experience of residential work in this impressive and authoritative work. His particular field of study consists of the 40 institutions that provide secure places for up to 3,000 disturbed or delinquent young people. Such figures conceal the true importance of these places and the young people who live in them. The daily population gives only the barest hint of the numbers who pass through these institutions in a decade. Each of them has the potential to become a stable, responsible and productive member of society, or to continue with a pattern of disruptive adolescent behaviour into an adulthood of confirmed criminality and broken relationships, at great and continuing cost to the rest of society. The influences to which residents are exposed during their periods of secure confinement must always be important, and may be critical, in determining which path is chosen.

Rose traces the history of the different strands that have come together in our present pattern of services, and locates their relationship within the wider patterns of residential child care and the different traditions of a prison service oriented towards adults. Throughout he emphasises the value of a regime that looks beyond physical security to address both the conduct that led to incarceration and the emotional damage that frequently precipitates it. He explores the characteristics that make rehabilitation a reality: a leadership committed to reform as well as to detain, management experienced and trained in the complex functions performed by secure institutions, and a multi-disciplinary staff trained in collaborative and inter-personal methods of work in a closed setting.

The history of this provision is not encouraging, including – as it does – inspired developments that could not be replicated, false starts based on a philosophy of deterrence, and partial successes that became obsolescent as they were overtaken by changes in the wider society. That society has consistently undervalued both the institutions and the staff who work in them, and perpetuates rejecting and punitive attitudes to their young inmates. Rose is frank about deficiencies in the system, and clear about what is needed to remedy them. There is cause for cautious optimism in the approach of the comparatively new Youth Justice Board, which appears to combine pragmatism with humanity. Cultural changes are needed at every level; this book makes substantial strides towards enabling them.

Sir William Utting
February 2002

*　*　*　*　*

In *Working with Young People in Secure Accommodation*, Jim Rose has achieved the near impossible, the encapsulation of his own immense experience in the field of secure care, within a context of current practice, policy, politics and the unique personal development of any young person in adversity.

Such young people arrive in secure accommodation after a series of diverse, damaging and disruptive experiences, ready to reinact their anger and despair with and indeed at times against staff. Those working in secure accommodation have, in turn, traditionally been undervalued and frequently criticised by the wider systems of social care, criminal justice and education.

In taking us on this journey of discovery, the special needs of gender, cultural, diversity and ethnicity are incorporated into a holistic needs led framework of care for each young person as they make the transition not only through their own challenges and difficulties but also through the process of adolescence, experienced in a locked setting.

Creating a healthy environment must include the 'listening' ear of case management; research including experiences as told by young people themselves.

The hardest and most important 'treatment' to deliver is the consistent provision and delivery of basic day-to-day care. Without this the 'expert' interventions whether it be offence specific or psychotherapeutic will falter and fail.

Jim Rose provides an excellent description and review of staff – staff, staff-young people and young people – young people's interactions and how these can be facilitated by a healthy physical building, good organisational and management structures, and informed and empowered relationships with inreach and outreach services as the young person moves on through and out of the secure setting.

Thus for those working within locked settings, this book will provide an invaluable source from which to draw knowledge, a way of approaching and living with young people and a point of strength and respite when an individual day has been especially difficult. However, this book should also be an essential read for all professionals who at any point in a child's development are involved in the decision-making process that leads to secure accommodation.

Jim Rose with great sensitivity demonstrates through his experience and the stories of young people, that whatever the circumstances, it is possible to provide a holistic approach to meet the developmental needs of a young person, including those who experience the transition of Chaos to Culture in secure accommodation.

Susan Bailey

Preface

Working with Young People in Secure Accommodation is neither an academic textbook nor a research thesis. It is a product of over twenty years of working with young people in residential care settings, including secure accommodation, and with many adults whom I have valued as colleagues. *Working with Young People in Secure Accommodation* describes how chaotic and disturbed young people may be helped during time spent in a secure unit and in particular through the relationships that they make with the residential staff who look after them in what is an intense and sometimes bewildering experience for both!

Above all *Working with Young People in Secure Accommodation* is written in recognition of the work done by those residential staff whose contribution to the outcomes achieved by young people is often un-acknowledged but is of vital importance. The day-to-day routines of group living are the main vehicles for shaping the overall environment of a secure unit and the arena in which relationships between adults and young people are formed. For many young people in secure units, the containment which comes from the predictable and reliable delivery of these routines and the ways in which they are encouraged to relate to adults offers them an experience of care different from anything they are likely to have known before. Recognising the therapeutic value of these 'ordinary' experiences and making sure that they are provided each day with the necessary knowledge, skill and enthusiasm is a real challenge but it is the core of the residential task.

If residential staff are helped to pursue this task with a greater under-standing, and managers and those outside secure units become better in-formed about what happens inside the walls, then *Working with Young People in Secure Accommodation* will have achieved its purpose. Where a case study is used, any details that might reveal the identity of a young person have been changed. This has been done to ensure confidentiality without detracting from the value of the material.

Acknowledgements

There are many adults and young people with whom I have worked over the years, from whom I have gained so much and without whom this book would not have been possible. However, there are some people without whose help and support this book could never have been written and to them special thanks are due. John Reid has given me invaluable advice throughout the period of writing as he has done so willingly over many years. His long experience and distinguished work with young people have been a source of guidance for me, as has his friendship. Thanks as well to Dr Earl Hopper who, by being utterly professional and at the same time wonderfully human, has helped me to develop the confidence to be myself. Alison, Joanna and Elizabeth were my own special children, then young people and now they are adults, of whom I am very proud and whom I love very much. Finally to Jean, without whose love and care I could not have kept this project going and who makes it all worthwhile.

Chapter 1

Introduction

'It's not going very well tonight is it?' It was indeed turning into one of those evening shifts dreaded by everyone who has worked in a children's residential home. Two staff had phoned in sick at the last minute and it felt more and more as if everyone else, and in particular the senior managers, had abandoned and deserted the unit. Two of us, both relatively inexperienced, were left to look after the resident group of eight young people, and as the evening went on our feelings of inadequacy and incompetence grew by the minute. We were working in a regional assessment centre for young people, although at times like these it felt as if survival rather than assessment was the key task. It was certainly our priority. I can't remember exactly what happened that night. In the great scheme of things I suppose nothing very dreadful went on, and even if it had we were so anxious we would probably have missed it.

You might imagine that the above were words of encouragement or support offered by my colleague; in fact they were spoken by Tom, one of the young people present in the unit during that shift. Twenty years later I still remember how they made me feel. Of course it wasn't just the words. It was the tone of his voice and the look on his face which, together with my already growing sense of being left alone and without support, made me feel so helpless. The idea that I should think about what Tom said to me or that it might provide some clues about how he was feeling never crossed my mind. In other words all the thoughts and emotions that were so troubling to me could have been used for the very purpose for which we were there, namely assessment! My difficulty was that in that moment I was not able to reflect on how Tom's comment might tell me something about him or in what ways my feeling of helplessness could be used to give some different meaning to the whole experience and thereby provide some learning for both of us. I can't really remember my reaction or what I said or did but I do remember the feeling of absolute despair that the situation engendered.

What is it about that experience twenty years on that makes me remember it so vividly? Although it was in many ways an insignificant event it is a typical example of what regularly happens in children's homes and secure units. Apparently trivial matters or disputes quickly acquire a huge significance and occupy the interest and attention of staff and young people for long periods of time. The smallest comment seemingly has the most wounding or the most profound effect. The key to understanding much of what goes on in residential settings is often found in the detail of the exchanges that take place between staff and staff, young person and young person or, perhaps most powerfully of all, between staff and young people. Sometimes staff may observe a piece of behaviour that does not make any sense at all until someone connects it to something that was said or done days or even weeks before. Of course these exchanges also have to be understood within the context of the different groups that make up a residential unit and to which each person relates. The dynamics of these groups have a continual and changing influence on the way relationships in the unit develop and therefore on the meaning of the encounters that take place between individuals. The brief exchange I had with Tom that night was like a single thread picked out of an entire blanket of events and relationships. My problem at that time, a result of my inexperience, was that I could not see or think beyond the immediate meaning and effect of the words. I could not connect that brief but wounding comment to anything that might have happened before, either in our relationship or in any other.

Purpose and aims

Working with Young People in Secure Accommodation is written to stimulate and encourage those who on a daily basis are involved in looking after young people in secure accommodation. I hope that the ideas and the practical examples used in the book will refresh their thinking and help them to re-examine their practice. Many people when appointed to work as residential staff in secure units are new to work with young people and have not had the benefit of professional training. They are very much put in 'at the deep end' and whether they sink or swim depends to a great extent on their own resourcefulness or, in the better scenarios, on the support they receive from colleagues and managers. Although managers of secure units tend to be more experienced in the practices of secure accommodation they often have little by way of induction or support when they take their tentative first steps into a management role. I hope that they too will find helpful material throughout this book and be able to use it to think more productively around the complex and onerous management responsibilities that they carry.

Working with Young People in Secure Accommodation is also intended for those who may have some external management responsibility for secure units or whose role in the wider systems of justice and welfare puts them in the position of referring and placing young people into conditions of security. In these positions it is essential to know something about what goes on inside secure units and to understand the way in which the dynamics of institutional life impact not just on staff and young people in the secure unit but also on those outside as well.

Working with Young People in Secure Accommodation is neither an academic textbook nor a research thesis. It is based on years of work in secure accommodation and draws on the shared experiences of staff and young people who have been together in those different environments. Good research and applied thinking, however, underpin the arguments put forward in the following chapters, and in no way should it be inferred that these are not important activities. References are made throughout the text to useful sources of information, research material and other literature, and further study of these is encouraged. Working with young people in a secure environment is both interesting and demanding. We shall see how important thinking is for day-to-day practice, and so any opportunity to read relevant books or articles should be gratefully taken, and managers are to be encouraged to develop structured approaches to the professional development of their staff groups. Issues of staff support and training are referred to constantly throughout the book and are explored in more detail in Chapter 8.

Many references are made in subsequent chapters to staff and young people, and in the main these terms are used inclusively without specifying either gender or ethnicity. The points that are made about the effects of working in a secure unit as a member of staff, or of being placed there as a young person, are of general application and relevance. In those instances when specific issues to do with young women or young people from minority ethnic backgrounds are being discussed, this is made clear. However, there are significant variations in the experience of these settings which come from the differences experienced as a result of race or gender (O'Neill 2001).

Almost every specific theme or topic discussed in the book can be viewed from the perspective of the needs of young women or young people from minority ethnic groups, and this should be borne in mind

throughout. Issues to do with primary care, management, regime programmes and activities each have a dimension in which individual matters of race, gender and culture are significant and should be taken into
account for the purposes of planning and provision in secure units. What
is it like to be a young black person or a girl in this unit, or a black female
member of staff? These are among the key questions that managers need
to be asking themselves constantly as they review the quality of life for
young people or the needs of their staff groups in the secure unit.

In the same way, issues for female staff also have a particular
significance in that the specific impact that both young men and young
women have on female staff has a definite and at times devastating quality about it. Often this is closely connected to the severe maternal deprivation that most of these young people have suffered, and as a result of
this they project especially strong feelings towards female staff. These
may be of a hostile and aggressive nature – most commonly experienced
from the girls in a unit – or they may be an expression of longing for some
sort of maternal affection, which comes mainly from the boys. In either
case the strength of the feelings from the young people and indeed of
those reciprocated by the female staff can be very strong and uncomfortable. Knowing and understanding about this and ensuring that female
staff are properly supported is a responsibility for managers, supervisors
and consultants. Too often, however, this is an area that goes unrecognised and therefore unacknowledged as a pressure point within a unit.
The predominantly male culture of secure units tends to emphasise a
more macho approach to dealing with feelings and may appear to be dismissive of more female qualities and ways of expressing experiences. In
an environment where issues of sexuality and sexual orientation are
inevitably always on the front burner, so to speak, there needs to be a
sensitive and thoughtful approach to dealing with such issues, and we
shall see the implications of this in a number of the case studies we consider later.

The underlying and fundamental principles of caring for young people
in secure units and the feelings, thoughts and emotions that this generates
are best considered within a holistic framework but, and this is the fascinating part of the process, as each individual is unique so every situation is
different and must be approached as such. Race, gender, culture and
religion are dimensions of individual identity and have to be understood
as elements, albeit crucial ones, in the story that a young person brings
with them and tells to the staff in the unit. This highlights yet another
aspect in residential group living: the importance of maintaining a balance between managing the group and meeting communal needs whilst at

the same time paying due care and attention to the individual needs of each young person.

Structure and content

The remainder of this introductory chapter is in two parts. First we shall look at the major themes of the book and how they are to be developed, and then consider in more detail the idea of the secure environment. The environment of a secure unit has both an internal and an external dimension. We need to think about how a secure unit works internally and what is required to make it a place in which staff and young people can work together to address the serious issues that face each young person. Secure units also have an external environment which needs to be understood and to some extent managed. The attitudes and views of those outside its walls, both professional groups and the wider public, have an impact on what goes on inside and on staff and young people.

The wider context

Although this book is in the main about the work that goes on inside secure units, and the ideas, human qualities and structures needed to sustain this, it is also necessary to consider the wider contexts in which secure units exist. In Chapter 2 we look at the way in which secure units have developed over the years and how social policies have shaped the provision of services. These changes often reflect the shifting and ambivalent views of the wider public about 'locking up young people' which in turn has a powerful effect on groups of staff and the young people who are placed in secure accommodation.

Also in Chapter 2 we consider in more detail some of the key factors that feature in the histories and backgrounds of young people who find themselves in a secure unit. It is important to know about these factors and understand something of the way in which they influence how those decisions which determine what happens to young people are made. A developmental perspective is deliberately taken in order to emphasise that young people admitted to secure units come with a history and have a future. It is also likely that the aetiology of their presenting disturbance and chaos can be traced and identified in the core of that developmental history.

There is another dimension to this perspective as well. Although the young people who are placed in secure accommodation are undoubtedly amongst the most damaged and disturbed in our society, they are also subject to the same processes of change that are experienced by every adolescent. Even in the best of circumstances the period of development known as adolescence brings with it special anxieties and worries, both for those going through it and for those who have responsibility for their care.

Adolescence is probably best defined as a time of transition from childhood to adulthood. Transitions have particular features involving change and readjustment to new conditions. As Ann Wheal puts it:

> As they pass through adolescence one can expect alternating times of calm and conflict. Each time a young person is prompted by a new opportunity to become more independent they may experience a surge of enthusiasm or excitement. Since they are facing a new and unfamiliar challenge, they may also feel afraid or overwhelmed. When this happens they may temporarily turn back to the old ways they used to cope as children. They may pout or throw a tantrum to get their own way or express frustration. They may withdraw and retreat or want someone to indulge, protect or comfort them. Just as toilet-trained children may suddenly lose their bowel and bladder control following the birth of a younger sibling teenagers too will regress to more childish levels of behaviour under the impact of strains or stress.
>
> (Wheal 1998: 5)

In their day-to-day work with young people in secure units it is essential that staff are able to distinguish between what may be described as 'normal' adolescent behaviour and manifestations of disturbed and delinquent behaviour which arise from the individual circumstances of a young person or are brought about as a result of being locked up in an institutional setting.

Staff also need knowledge about the world in which young people are growing up and the differences between today and yesterday. Although it is helpful for adults who work with young people to be aware of their own experiences as adolescents and of the kinds of feelings and opinions they had as a young person, they also have to be aware of the changes that have occurred in society over recent years. Of course the age of staff will be relevant here and many older staff have had the experience of already bringing up their own children through the period of adolescence. Being exposed to working with young people in custody may be very challenging for this group of staff as their contact with the young people makes them recall and reflect on how they were as parents to their own children.

For younger staff the pressures are different but no less real. For them the issues may be much more to do with recalling their more recent experiences of being parented and of coming to terms with adult authority in a mature way. Younger staff who are still acting out their own adolescent rebellion, or older staff reliving theirs, are not uncommon features of life in secure units. More than any other group, adolescents evoke powerful feelings in those who work closely with them. Having an awareness of these feelings and being able to understand and manage them are essential for effective working. It is also why the optimism we have previously described as essential for this work is justified. Holding on to the belief that adolescents can and do change is critical, for, after all, this is the very definition of what adolescence is all about although for long periods of time, when the same behaviour occurs over and over again, it doesn't seem like it! As someone wisely once put it: when adolescents are being children it is all right because you can nurture them; when they are being adult it is all right because you can talk to them rationally; but when they are being adolescents it is impossible!

The importance of thinking

Working with Young People in Secure Accommodation takes ideas seriously and in Chapter 3 we consider a number of ideas which although originating in different disciplines have direct relevance to and bearing on work in secure units. Ideas are important because they provide helpful reference points when facing some bewildering event or trying to make sense of something that seems barely rational or out of kilter with what might usually be expected. These are constant features of life in secure units where people work closely together in often stressful situations and are tasked with looking after disturbed young people. Odd things happen; people behave in ways that are unexpected; feelings emerge, often of a violent or sexual nature, that you thought you would never have or had long buried; you find yourself wanting to do or say something that you barely believe you are capable of. Sometimes these sorts of thoughts and feelings cannot be acknowledged. In some instances it may not be safe even to admit feeling a bit unsure about something, let alone to admit feeling murderous towards someone or to talk about the sexual tension in the staff and young people's group at the moment! But these are the feelings whose content, if discussed carefully and sensibly, is able to provide so much information about what is going on either within the group or with a particular young person. They also offer reassurance to a worried member of staff that they are not going mad or turning into a psychopath!

Having a tool box of ideas which can provide some help to explore these feelings in neutral but explanatory language is critical.

To make ideas work you need to be able to think, and yet providing time and opportunity for staff to think does not often figure greatly in the key targets or performance indicators for most organisations. However, it could be argued that thinking is perhaps one of the most critical tasks for staff. When we discuss the idea of containment in more detail we shall see how the important principle of 'holding in the mind' requires staff to think about the young people in their care and how this in turn contributes to their well-being. Ideas are not just important for helping to make sense of the 'here and now', although this is the locus for much of the residential worker's dealings with young people; they are also the framework for understanding human development and for building models to show how experiences connect and make sense on the larger scale.

The views of young people

Listening and taking into account the views of young people have become a recognised part of most of the formal casework processes in both welfare and justice systems. We shall see how case management meetings in secure units are designed to encourage participation by young people and their families, and how in day-to-day activities the positive involvement of young people contributes enormously to creating a healthy environment.

Although the intention at policy level is clear about the involvement of young people there are still huge issues as to how effectively in practice this participation is allowed to happen. In Chapter 4 we look at some research into this important area and also consider in detail the particular experiences of two young people who spent long periods in secure units.

Focus on practice

Chapters 5, 6 and 7 are in many respects the core chapters of *Working with Young People in Secure Accommodation* as they directly address issues of day-to-day practice in secure units and what managers are required to do in order for this work to be effective. The way in which daily work routines are organised and the manner in which staff perform their duties are critical factors in determining the overall outcome of the time spent by a young person in secure accommodation. A recurring theme, therefore, throughout these chapters is the importance of the consistent provision and delivery of reliable basic primary care by a staff team who understand its significance. This is the bedrock upon which more sophisticated interventions are built.

The way in which relationships may be used as a focus for a young person's programme and how they are best managed organisationally are also considered in some detail and from different perspectives. Relationships between staff and young people are formed and developed by sharing in those ordinary day-to-day events and routines which are the life-blood of residential work. The ordinary daily exchanges and conversations, the shared humour, pain, frustration, excitement and despair that being together in this setting brings, are not peripheral or by-products of the core task. They are integral elements for understanding the ways in which residential care can provide a healthy and creative experience for young people.

The provision of a high-quality residential experience in secure accommodation does not just happen and is not easy to achieve. It requires a well-planned organisational and management structure firmly founded on sound thinking and coherent ideas about the nature of the task. This is why it is necessary to consider carefully the work of managers in a secure unit and what resources they need in order to properly fulfil their responsibilities.

For all of the above to happen depends on the kind of environment created within a secure unit and the nature of the predominant culture which influences how staff think about their work and behave towards each other and the young people in their care. It is to this issue that we now turn.

The secure environment

The inherent challenges for the institutions and staff who look after and manage this group of young people are complex and many-faceted. The developmental histories of many of the young people mean that the design and management of the living environment have to take their disturbance and its potential risks into account, so that the physical space of the secure unit and the social and emotional environments which the staff provide come together to ensure sufficient containment and safety. For those young people in particular who may do a significant part of their growing up in a secure unit it is essential that the overall environment in which they are living is organised in such a way that the proper conditions exist for healthy physical, emotional and psychological growth to occur. This is why, despite considerable investment and some excellent new facilities, the conditions that prevail inside much of the residential accommodation in prison service establishments make the proper implementation of the planned-for changes in regime more difficult to achieve.

Relationships between staff and young people

Although the design and equipping of the physical environment play a big part in a young person's overall experience, the most important feature of the environment, and ultimately the most containing, is the quality of the relationships established by the adult group in their day-to-day dealings with the young people. Research shows how healthy child development and growth occur primarily through the relationship that an individual child has with its parents. Most children experience 'good enough' parenting which prepares them to take their place in the world, establish an individual identity, feel reasonably good about themselves most of the time and develop personal relationships that provide a satisfactory degree of fulfilment and pleasure. Such is most unlikely to be the case for the young people who find themselves in secure units. Research again tells us that their early experiences of parental figures are likely to have been characterised by combinations of inconsistency in care, neglect and abuse, which are perpetrated, in some instances, over long periods of time. Indeed throughout their entire growing up these are young people who have had difficulties in forming relationships and who have found adults to be generally untrustworthy. Such young people often present as chaotic, hostile, destructive and antisocial. They may be prone to self-harming, aggression or extreme delinquency. They have generally under-achieved in education, have very low self-esteem and probably have experienced a number of social work or other types of intervention. If the fundamental disorder of these young people is to be addressed it is essential that their experience of adults whilst they are in a secure unit should be significantly different from before. Despite their previous experience, adults continue to matter to young people and this can be seen in secure units in the way young people constantly seek adult attention. Although there may be barriers to overcome there are very few young people who do not in some way respond to such attention when it is offered positively. Irrespective of their professional background the adult staff group needs to be able to provide a consistency of approach which is underpinned by respect and a willingness to reflect upon their thoughts, feelings, reactions and judgements regarding the behaviour and attitudes of the young people. It is by thinking about and processing individual reactions that a staff group begins to move towards an attitude which helps to set boundaries and yet at the same time offers care, compassion and understanding.

Daily life

An important aspect of this approach is the ability of the staff to set clear expectations about what is acceptable and unacceptable behaviour, and to establish and maintain boundaries around these. This links to the importance of the experience of secure care for young people as being one in which they can be sure that the adults in the placement are able to tolerate their behaviour, hold on through difficult times to the material which they are presenting and believe that change and growth are possible despite what has gone before. In all secure units the relationships between young people and adults are formed primarily through the day-to-day sharing of the routines that emerge naturally through the process of group living. These include key events such as getting up and having breakfast, going to education or work programmes, eating meals together, group activities and going to bed. Within this sharing of daily routines, opportunities can be shaped in small group meetings to help young people to think about what is happening around them and to give and receive feedback about their involvement in group life. In this context of group living there is another important element that adds significantly to the ability of the adult group to contain young people and help their development. This is the provision of high levels of adult attention to the particular and individual needs of each young person in the group. It is critically important for each young person to know that at some level they are being thought about positively and held in the mind of the group of adults responsible for their care, and in particular in the minds of key adult figures involved in their daily programme.

The needs of staff

In creating an environment that can provide enough safety to engage and challenge the young people's group, staff are required to immerse themselves in the day-to-day world of extremely damaged and disturbed young people, to offer a stimulating range of activities and experiences and to establish individual and group relationships that from time to time feel overwhelming. Paying careful attention to the needs of the staff groups who work with these young people and helping them to acquire the necessary knowledge and skills are essential if they are to feel supported and able to go on providing for such a demanding group. Creating the kind of environment in which the importance of providing this level of support for staff is acknowledged and in which it can happen safely requires strong management. In their daily work, managers of secure units have to confront an unusually wide range of issues, so it is vital that they too feel that they are working in a supportive environment. In order to manage a secure unit effectively managers must be in touch with the 'emotional realities' of the organisation. In practice this means having the capacity to understand and contain the extraordinarily high levels of anxiety that such institutions generate. This anxiety emerges mainly from the complex dynamics of the multiple relationships that exist within and outside of the organisational boundary. Secure units are located within an intricate network of external authorities who provide management, inspection and regulation on an ever-increasing scale. Managers have to contain not only the anxieties of people who work within their institution but also the anxieties carried by those outside its perimeter walls. This includes not only people who work for official bodies, because the local and general public also have strong views about the 'goings on' inside locked institutions and their feelings are likely to be highly ambivalent. Apparent conflicts between punishment and rehabilitation or care and control set up all sorts of moral dilemmas with which society constantly wrestles but which it somehow has never resolved. It is a major challenge for managers to manage staff groups in a way that is able to contain the pressures that come upon the institution from both within and without, so that anxieties are contained and staff are thereby freed up to pursue their daily work alongside a disturbed and challenging young people's group. Of course they cannot be expected to do this on their own. It is essential that they receive understanding and support from their own managers, as well as having regular access to other professionals from disciplines such as psychology or psychiatry whose knowledge and skills can be made available for the purposes of making sense of events and feelings within the institution.

The external world

Secure units are subject to much confused thinking about their role and purpose: to control and punish or to care and promote change? Justice or welfare? At different times these aims have been put in conflict against each other and different priorities have been set for the care and management of young people who have presented antisocial behaviours. This polarisation has resulted in a real ambivalence in society's responses to the problems and challenges presented by recalcitrant children, and ongoing confusion in the minds of professional agencies and their staff.

In 1853 there were around 12,000 children in prison. Today, the total population of children and young people in all forms of secure accommodation in England and Wales is around 3,000. Although it may be argued from these figures that over the years the welfare needs of children have become increasingly pre-eminent, many would argue that the current number of young people locked up is far too large, and, proportionate to population, it certainly puts the UK towards the top of the list amongst first world countries in terms of the rates of incarceration of its young.

Society's ambivalence is further illustrated by the fact that it is the prison service which is by far the largest provider of secure accommodation for young people under the age of 18 years. Astonishingly it is only since 1999 that this service has made any real acknowledgement that the needs of young people in this age group require a different kind of regime from that provided for its majority adult population. Responses in the media to the way young people are treated in secure units are also indicative of a wider ambivalence. On the one hand there is always an outcry, rightly so, when poor conditions are exposed. On the other hand there never seems to be a shortage of stories about 'holiday camps'. Certain notorious cases always attract extraordinarily high levels of media coverage – the debate about the appropriate sentence length for the two young people who murdered James Bulger, and in what conditions this should have been served, demonstrates the point all too clearly. The purpose here is not to get into the rights and wrongs of these various debates but to note that they are going on, that they are always conducted with a tremendous emotional charge and that scant regard is generally paid to any kind of research or evaluative work.

The impact of this ambivalence seeps right through into the functioning of secure units themselves and can have a debilitating and damaging effect on the work of the staff groups in them. These professionals often perceive the value of their work as being subject to criticism and consequently may be prone to regard almost any external viewpoint as intrusive and with suspicion. This is a potentially dangerous situation because what goes on behind the locked doors of a secure unit must be open to scrutiny and inspection and their regimes transparent and clearly articulated.

There is yet another dimension to all this, which is that the widespread ambivalence, of which the staff are aware and maybe to some extent share, is also well known to the young people themselves. To a greater or lesser extent they too have some sense of the low regard with which they are regarded by society outside the institution, and this may serve only to exacerbate their already low self-esteem, making them even more resentful and disaffected.

It is certainly the case, however, that unless a secure unit establishes a clear framework of thinking and practice which is understood and accepted by the staff groups working within it then the problems and difficulties of young people will not be properly managed or their needs responded to. The same applies to the wider systems and professional agencies working outside the secure unit. The models of practice used by secure units also, of course, have to be acceptable to the wider policy-making authorities external to the unit. Indeed the current political agenda determines how secure units are defined in terms of their purpose and function. Recent research demonstrates how unless there is a clear statement of purpose in residential care settings, including secure accommodation, which brings together the expressed wider and external aims of a residential unit with the way staff understand and carry out their work inside, then the resulting conflict will inevitably create a weak and ineffective regime (Bullock *et al.* 1998). In other words, the culture of a residential unit must have at its core a clear understanding of the reasons why it is there and what it is trying to achieve. This is, as we have seen, particularly difficult for a secure unit whose function sharply focuses the inherent ambivalence of society about how young people in secure accommodation should be regarded and treated.

From chaos to culture

The idea of a transition from chaos to culture is intended to denote a process of change from a state of confusion and disorder to one in which sense and order can be defined and experienced. This process of transition may be thought about in terms of individuals, groups or whole organisations but it is never linear or straightforward. We shall see how the chaotic internal worlds of the young people in secure units are often mirrored and acted out in the external relationships between the adults involved in their care and management. If a young person is to be enabled to understand their chaos and to become more settled and stable in their behaviour and ways of relating to the world around them, they first need to experience an environment which offers predictability, safety and consistency. The culture of a secure unit is expressed through its routines, structures and ritualised ways of dealing with both good and bad events and circumstances. The culture as such, however, is primarily identified and experienced by the young people in the nature and quality of the relationships they form with adults in that environment.

It is the argument of this book that the aim of time spent in secure accommodation is to help a young person to begin to internalise the external culture which they experience through the daily routines of the residential unit in which they are living, and so become more able to make choices and decisions about how to be responsible for their own behaviour. This is the practical outcome of the transition from chaos to culture, and it is also the context within which the current expressed aim of the youth justice system, to prevent offending, may be best understood and is most likely to be made effective.

Making a transition from chaos to culture is not achieved by the rigid imposition of rules and regulations, hoping that if only we could have more control over people or events then chaos would be eliminated. It is achieved through struggling to make space for thinking so that informed decisions can be made, even if only about what to do next. For each individual young person the chaos of their life is what gives shape to the order being sought, because the process is about making sense of earlier experience in order to live more fruitfully in the future. Of course, to help that process develop, routine and structure are essential but they are a means to an end: the creation of a safe and secure space in which young people can be encouraged to find opportunities for growth and change.

Balancing the complex demands that arise in working in secure accommodation with young people is not easy. I certainly did not manage it on that evening shift twenty years ago. I did not have any idea that the chaos I was experiencing or the feelings I had might have become tools to produce some very different outcomes and learning. I hope that *Working with Young People in Secure Accommodation* will help others to avoid that mistake and be able to offer more to the young people for whom they care.

Chapter 2

Setting the scene

Past and to come seems best; things present, worst.
(Shakespeare, *Henry IV Part 2*, I.iii)

The maelstrom of daily life in secure units is the background to many of the discussions in the following pages, but before stepping into this world it is necessary to take a few steps back. We have already acknowledged that in residential work with children and young people the smallest details and events of daily life may acquire a disproportionate significance. However, the importance of this detail is only truly understood when it is given its place on a larger canvas and becomes part of the whole picture. Similarly, the different and wider contexts in which work in secure units takes place have also to be identified. This means paying some attention to the links between the social policies which have shaped current provision and practice, the historical processes from which these have emerged and the intellectual traditions which have informed their development. For our purposes the strands of social policy, history and intellectual tradition need to be woven together so that we may see more clearly how society has chosen over the years to look after its most needy and delinquent children and young people.

There are those who will want to dispute the value of writing this kind of book at all, those for whom residential work and secure units are anathema. In the UK, unlike in other countries in Europe such as Denmark (Madge 1994), there is no great status or kudos to be gained by embarking on a career in residential work with children and young people. Indeed, it is highly arguable whether in any sense it is meaningful to talk about a career in residential work. Remaining positive about the value of this kind of work and what may be achieved with children and young people through group living could easily be thought of as naive or, even worse, indicative of some sort of deep perversion. It is not uncommon to hear the view expressed that residential child care and in particular secure units, in the wider sense with which we are using the term, are inherently abusive to young people. The scandals and abuse which have been so prevalent throughout this sector of work, and which have stained almost every type of institutional care for ill, damaged and needy people, are well documented. It is right to confront and expose these scandals and the evils that they represent. It is also true that the standard of much of what currently passes as secure accommodation for young people, particularly in the prison service, is unacceptable and requires radical and fundamental overhaul.

Working with Young People in Secure Accommodation is, however, unashamedly positive about the value of residential work and the potential benefits that it can provide for young people, whilst at the same time readily acknowledging its inherent problems. There have been a number of serious consequences arising from the persistent and critical attacks on residential care over recent years. In general terms the significantly reduced number of residential homes for young people has meant that there is now a limited choice of placements available for young people who, for whatever reason, cannot live at home with their natural family. Not all of these young people want to be fostered and a proportion actually prefer the option of residential care. For staff, including those working in secure units, there have been dramatic impacts on morale and increasing problems of recruitment and retention. In residential work, more than in any other kind of therapeutic activity, to be successful in the struggle to hold on to people who are bent on a course of self-destruction or acting dangerously towards others, there has to be the will to do it. To have that will to go on and not give up in the face of sometimes overwhelming odds requires the belief that the endeavour is intrinsically worthwhile. Being optimistic but at the same time realistic about what can be achieved in any given situation should almost be regarded as essential for doing this work. For many young people, whose own faith in themselves has been shot to pieces through years of being let down or abused, it has been the presence of an adult group prepared and determined to hold on and stay with them that has made the difference. This is the experience of many young people and adults in residential care settings including secure units.

It may well be the case that too many young people are locked up in this country and that a good number of those in secure units could be better dealt with through an increased or better-resourced range of community-based services. On the other hand it is also the case that there are a small number of young people who need and benefit from the containment and care that are provided by conditions of security. In any case it is undeniably true that the only area of residential child care where there is any planning for expansion over the next few years is secure accommodation. Given that there is a continuing societal and political demand for this type of intervention, as well as potential therapeutic benefit, it is surely more profitable on balance to focus the debates around how this type of care is best provided rather than whether or not it should be. If so, then it follows that greater attention must be paid to ways of identifying the essential ingredients that must be included in the regimes and programmes provided by secure units so that they can provide as positive an experience as possible for young people and achieve the goals set for them by wider society. More research of this kind would support current efforts being made to ensure that the issues raised in the investigations of past abuses are addressed, and that regimes which provide opportunities for change, education and personal development are delivered and sustained. At the same time it is important to establish credible programmes for the evaluation of these regimes and to monitor the outcomes of all interventions for young people.

The references and suggestions for further reading at the end of this book point readers towards certain books which give more detailed accounts of the themes we have discussed above. These are important reading and will help in developing a wider frame of reference within which to consider the current role of secure units as part of the continuum of services for young people who present problems for themselves or society as a whole. The task in this instance is to identify a few of the key points that emerge from these fields of study and to use them to support our central purpose, i.e. to inform our understanding of what goes on in secure units and how this affects staff and young people.

An historical perspective

In taking an historical perspective to look at how social policies have changed with regard to the treatment of problematic young people, and linking these to the way different traditions in residential child care have developed over the years, a clear tension emerges between two prominent themes: the need for social control and the promotion and improvement of conditions for the welfare of children. Even a cursory study shows how in different eras the pendulum seems to have swung first one way and then the other. The history of legislation in this area similarly illustrates how at certain times attempts have been made to hold the two together, whilst in other periods pieces of legislation clearly emphasise one aspect or the other. In their *Evaluation of Medway Secure Training Centre*, Ann Hagell and colleagues draw attention to this and also show how these emphases are often dependent on broader social or economic factors which influence the way in which society attempts to solve perceived problems concerning its young.

> The need to control a small group of very persistent or recalcitrant children is perennial. Evidence of specific methods of doing so have been available since at least the 18th century, particularly coinciding with the industrial revolution and the movement of families from rural to urban contexts. In the cities, some children were more obviously identified as out of control. Prison was a way of imposing control and threatening the liberty of those contemplating behaving in an antisocial way.
>
> (Hagell *et al.* 2000: 1)

And later:

> From time to time there has been a reaction against the zeal to control and imprison. Against the background of repeated waves of concern about youth crime there has been a long series of attempts to abolish or reduce powers to imprison children, to restrict the time that they can spend in prison, or to provide more benign places for them to go .... Welfare was a mechanism for releasing children from control and the two philosophies have co-existed rather uneasily ever since.
>
> (ibid.: 2)

It is possible to study the development of residential child care provision by using a similar control–welfare paradigm. The history of custodial institutions, when traced through prisons, Borstals, Detention Centres, Youth Custody Centres and Young Offender Institutions, may be linked to the growth of what seem rather hybrid institutions such as Approved Schools, Community Homes with Education and, more recently, Secure Training Centres. The origin of local authority secure units dates from the early 1960s and they form part of the Approved Schools tradition. These institutions were abolished in the sweeping changes brought about by the 1969 Children and Young Persons Act and were replaced by Community Homes with Education, (CHEs), a number of which included secure accommodation. At this point these units became the responsibility of social service departments and, along with the development of the Youth Treatment Service, managed centrally by the Department of Health, were initially intended to provide support to welfare services for the most difficult and disturbed of children, but also included in their population young people who were convicted of the most serious offences.

Most Community Homes with Education have now been closed, although the secure accommodation facilities attached to them have often remained and stand alone as secure units. Rarely, however, is the custodial tradition linked to the general history of children's residential homes and in particular to that tradition of establishments whose purpose has been more overtly therapeutic. Interestingly a number of these types of homes developed their therapeutic role in the course of transforming themselves from custodial institutions. An example of an institution changing its purpose through a complete change of ethos is the Peper Harow Community, which emerged from the experience of the Park House Approved School and whose story is told in a compelling and fascinating way by Melvyn Rose in *Healing Hurt Minds* (M. Rose 1990).

It is not immediately clear why the different traditions about how to look after difficult children and young people have remained so apart, because the population of children and young people placed in all types of institution share many of the same characteristics and problems. Even a cursory study of recent writing about practice issues in children's residential care reveals how similar the issues are and how the lessons learned in the experience of working residentially with disturbed children could equally apply to the development of sound practices in the secure estate (Kahan 1994, Burton 1993). There has been little in the way of cross-fertilisation, which would have been the case if staff moved as a matter of course from one area of work to another. Even today there are few opportunities for sharing information about the differences and similarities of work with young people in these diverse settings, and the relative isolation of the professional groups within them is striking. Prison officers know little about how residential social workers perform their tasks and vice versa. More may be known about each other's work by staff in Young Offender Institutions and local authority secure units, but it is most unlikely that a prison officer will know anything about how a member of staff in a larger therapeutic unit would be encouraged to respond to a situation or understand a piece of behaviour. In later chapters we shall see how the application of many of the principles of what constitutes good child care practice in a residential setting may be applied to the work undertaken even in those secure units that have a solely custodial role.

The youth justice system

Reform of the youth justice system has been a major policy feature of the government's legislative programme since 1997. These reforms have been spearheaded by the Youth Justice Board, a non-governmental agency established to co-ordinate and deliver the government's policies for youth justice, and which as part of its overall function has since April 2000 assumed full responsibility for young people sentenced to custody in England and Wales.

One of the priority tasks for the Youth Justice Board has been the creation of a national framework of Youth Offending Teams. The statutory membership of these teams includes education and health services along with social services, police and probation. Youth Offending Teams are accountable to the Chief Executive of each local authority, and it is the intention that this arrangement should bring about a more consistent approach in providing services for those young people who become caught up in the youth justice system. This must also mean a greater sharing of resources and easier access to the specialist services that are required to meet the wide spectrum of needs that this group of young people presents.

Links between Youth Offending Teams and secure units have also been redefined in these changes, mainly through legislative requirements in the implementation of the Detention and Training Order which was introduced in the Crime and Disorder Act of 1998. This is now the order for the vast majority of young people who receive a custodial order in England and Wales. The structure of the order lays an equal emphasis on the first half of the sentence which is spent in custody and the second half which is served in the community. Sentence planning, which begins whilst the young person is in custody, must take account of the two parts of the sentence and, from the initial planning stage onwards, include recommendations, targets and action plans for the period in the community. The Training Plan, therefore, has to be a joint piece of work between the custodial setting and the Youth Offending Team who have responsibility for the young person on their release into the community. This joint approach to planning, now firmly located within the structure of the sentence, goes a long way to breaking down the historical barriers between staff in secure units and community-based workers. In a similar fashion the guidelines for the implementation of the Detention and Training Order set out a number of expectations about the involvement of the young person and their family throughout the course of the sentence. The focus of the Training Plan is a series of targets for young people to achieve which are aimed at preventing re-offending and reintegration into the community. Young people who achieve particularly well on these targets may be eligible for early release. The Training Plan is the vehicle for planning a young person's programme whilst serving a Detention and Training Order sentence, but it is only part of a wider series of assessments and reports which provide a fuller picture of their needs and patterns of offending behaviour.

The introduction of the ASSET documentation standardises the assessment process for young people in relation to offending behaviour, and for the first time a common approach is now being taken to recording a young person's needs and the factors influencing their criminal activity. The ASSET document is regularly updated and accompanies a young person through their ongoing involvement with the various agencies. Other key documents introduced include Post Court Reports and Vulnerability Assessments, which are intended to ensure that accurate information passes between different agencies and in particular that information about the potential vulnerability of a young person entering custody is readily accessible and available to staff undertaking the admissions process.

The other groups of young people looked after in secure units who are placed there as a result of involvement in the youth justice system are those remanded by the courts and those sentenced under Section 91 of the Powers of the Criminal Courts (Sentencing) Act 2000. The latter has replaced the well-known Section 53 Order and is used for detaining young people who are convicted of serious offences which carry a sentence of fourteen years or more in the adult court. It is the remand population, however, that has occasioned much concern. These are in many respects the most vulnerable of the secure unit population. The period of time to be spent in a secure unit is often of an undetermined length as a result of the uncertainties as to how long court processes will go on, and their status as unconvicted 'prisoners' can produce ambiguities in their treatment as young people in need of care and education. The development of a more coherent approach to the case management of this group of young people and of a common standard in what services they should receive in secure units will help to improve the level of care that they receive whilst away from home during a very stressful period of their lives.

The described changes to the way services are organised will inevitably take time to have their intended effect on the scale envisaged and for a uniform high standard of work to be achieved. Initial difficulties that have been experienced generally arise from the varying degrees to which the vision of the reforms has been embraced from area to area, and the extent to which the different agencies required to participate have been prepared to invest the necessary level of resources. These changes and new practices are in many ways really only confirming what has always been seen as good practice, but they are now encompassed as statutory requirements.

Other problems that have been encountered include the long distances at which some young people are placed from their families, which inevitably limits the level of involvement by Youth Offending Teams in casework during the custodial period; and the fact that all staff need to become accustomed to using a standard set of forms, the proper completion of which places more demands on staff time than was previously the case. Although the structure of the Training Plan is undoubtedly more beneficial to young people, the additional staff time for involvement in casework planning has to be taken into account and has resource implications for managers. In many respects it is probably prison service staff who have been most affected by the increased casework required for each young person serving a Detention and Training Order. It is not just an increase in the number of casework meetings, however, that is a challenge to the prison service. The format of the Training Plan and the necessity of planning for the community phase of the sentence make explicit the requirement for an integrated multi-disciplinary and multi-agency approach to the programme for each young person. Although the prison service is well-used to staff working in multi-disciplinary teams, the concept of delivering an integrated programme for a young person on a day-to-day basis, which includes a caseworking input from prison officers, presents more of a challenge. For young people in secure accommodation it is not just the formal elements of a regime that count but the total experience that they have of life within the unit. Working from this model and then translating that into a coherent set of casework reports which reflect the totality of a young person's period in custody is a real challenge for the prison service. Improvements and advances are being made, however, as the distinct needs of this group of young people are being increasingly recognised through the experience of having to manage them as a separate group and in responding to the requirements of the Youth Justice Board.

Integrated planning is particularly important in ensuring that a young person's transition to the community, and most likely back to their family, is as well supported as possible. In the main it is the responsibility of Youth Offending Teams to provide for this transition, and their struggle to allocate the proper level of resources needed to deliver the programme is a source of considerable frustration for them and for staff in secure units.

The secure estate

A Youth Justice Task Force, convened by the Home Office in 1998, reported that 'different types of facilities for young people in the juvenile estate are in need of major reform'. This report concluded a review of the whole estate of secure facilities for young people, and far-reaching changes in the way secure units are managed and funded are amongst the consequences. It was intended that the outcomes of this review would result in a more co-ordinated use of secure accommodation for young people, with common standards of care and practice being delivered by all providers in the local authority, prison service and independent sectors. The report highlighted a number of serious deficiencies:

> Current arrangements are inconsistent and unsatisfactory. Young Offender Institutions are too large. Bullying and abuse of one offender by another occurs too often while education offered is poor. Some YOIs have made major efforts to provide good services, but even in these there is scope for improving links between supervision received inside the institution and in the community. By comparison, local authority secure units are often very small but with high unit costs. Resources are used inconsistently. Offenders in council units have the costs of education, health and accommodation paid for by their council and the National Health Service, while the costs of YOIs are borne by the Prison Service. There would be advantage in local health and education services being responsible for all offenders in the secure estate. This would reinforce links with local communities and produce more consistent funding. There is a strong case for funding following the young person. This would provide an incentive for local areas to provide robust non-custodial sentences. There needs to be more consistent unit costs in a narrower range – not to be uniform but reflecting different needs, including those of younger and more vulnerable offenders for additional care and support.
>
> (Youth Justice Task Force Report 1998)

Many of the issues raised in this report have become the agenda for the work of the Youth Justice Board as it has assumed its responsibilities for the management of the secure estate. As part of its review of the year 1999–2000 the Board defined its role with regard to secure accommodation for young people as follows:

The Youth Justice Board has responsibility for reforming conditions for young offenders in custody. It will ensure that time is well spent so that when a young person is released they do not continue to offend and have the skills necessary to build constructive lives. Every institution holding young people will have to demonstrate to the Board that they are implementing new national standards. Vulnerable young offenders will be placed in appropriate institutions and the Board will ensure that they are placed as close as possible to their homes. The new sentence for young offenders – the Detention and Training Order – will mean that offenders will serve their sentences half in custody and half under the supervision of the Youth Offending Team in the community. Achieving continuity between both elements of the sentence is vital to preventing further offending.

(Youth Justice Board 2000)

Throughout this book the term secure units is used generically to describe local authority secure accommodation, Young Offender Institutions and secure training centres. At the beginning of the year 2002 there were three independently managed secure training centres providing some 120 places, twenty-four local authority secure units contracted with the Youth Justice Board to provide around 320 places, and thirteen prison service establishments providing around 2,500 places. Where a specific type of secure unit is being discussed this is made clear in the text, especially when, later on, consideration is given to the differences between types of institution and their varying roles.

The different types of secure unit have grown out of separate traditions and this is reflected in the diverse ethoses that exist in each of them. Local authority secure units are managed by social service departments and about 30 per cent of places in these units are for young people not subject to any criminal order. These children and young people are placed as part of a process of social work decision making and planning on the grounds of their need for protection and safety, which is supported by a legal order in the Family Court under the Children Act 1989. These are young people who may present extreme levels of self-harming or other antisocial behaviours. Managing the mix of young people placed under different legal orders is a particular problem for these units. Although the needs of these young people are very similar, there are inevitable management differences that arise from their legal status, not least in the perceptions of the young people themselves about their reasons for being in secure accommodation and what should be the nature of their care (O'Neill 2001).

However, the population of young offenders in secure training centres and Young Offender Institutions also presents along a broad continuum of similar needs to those placed in local authority secure units, and the development of effective programmes for their care, management, education and treatment has to take into account their diverse histories and experiences. Many of these young people have mental health problems and their experience of adults throughout their young lives has been seriously distorted through ill-treatment and abuse. Although there may be a widespread range of needs in the young people's groups, there is at least a shared reason for being there, i.e. a decision of a court in relation to an offence having been, or alleged to have been, committed. Of course this can disguise huge differences that exist between young people, arising from differences in the types of offences they have committed, their previous offending histories and the length of sentence they are serving.

The Youth Justice Board has set as one of its key aims in the area of secure accommodation for young people under 18 years the achievement of common standards and programmes across the whole of the secure estate. This is a laudable aim, particularly if it includes a redistribution or at least an equalising of investment and capital spends between the local authority and prison service parts of the estate. Making everything the same is not necessarily the best way forward, of course. The distinctive and particular role that different sectors or units within them can play needs to be more fully explored, particularly in relation to the identified and known needs of young people. Common standards only take you so far in this, although they are important at a time when there is such a marked variation between establishments.

Routes into secure accommodation

Secure units are integral to those parts of the complex criminal justice and social welfare systems that relate to children and young people. Their specific functions place them right at the heart of the ambivalence we have already alluded to in the apparently conflicting aims of those systems: providing acceptable levels of social control and identifying and meeting welfare needs. An examination of the different roles played by the multitude of social, educational and justice agencies with which a young person may come into contact shows how these systems overlap. As problems increase and behaviour becomes harder to manage, more and more agencies are likely to become involved before a placement is finally made in a secure unit. Which particular agency first becomes involved with a child or young person may well determine their subsequent route into some form of secure accommodation. This initial contact often depends on the situation in which the behaviour of the child or young person first comes to notice. Dr Susan Bailey makes the point that young people with severe problems – often those with a mental health component and who are a danger to themselves or others – may come to the attention of any number of agencies but find that their mental health needs are not well recognised, widely understood or adequately met (Kurtz *et al.* 1998). The authors of *Secure Treatment Outcomes*, who are members of the Dartington Social Research Unit, identify various 'career paths' for that very small group of adolescents who, because of the extreme behavioural problems they display, consume a wholly disproportionate amount of available social welfare resources. This group, following along these different pathways, eventually find themselves placed in secure accommodation. According to the Dartington study, the careers of these most difficult young people may be tracked along one of the following paths: experience of long-term state care or special education; a very serious one-off offence; serious and persistent offending; or the phenomenon of the 'adolescent erupter', i.e. those young people who only come to the attention of agencies in early or mid-adolescence and then pass rapidly through the system into secure accommodation. They also identify that the characteristics of these groups of young people are not uniform, which is important when it comes to planning services and interventions:

> The young people in secure treatment centres are clearly a very heterogeneous group. Although they meet the criteria for placement in terms of disorder and danger in all other aspects they are very varied .... As a group they display a higher than expected rate for almost every disadvantage and behavioural difficulty. However, no single characteristic dominates the population.
>
> (Bullock *et al.* 1998: 46)

Plotting the factors that contribute to the reasons why a young person goes down one pathway rather than another provides valuable information about the way different systems operate and the kind of decision making that contributes to particular outcomes being achieved. The context in which a child's problems are first identified inevitably defines the model and vocabulary for understanding and explicating the nature of their difficulties. Professionals 'on the ground' often bemoan the lack of co-ordination of service provision at higher levels and the difficulties of accessing the right resources at the right time for needy young people. Problems of communication between professional agencies are also commonplace. Government policy since 1997 has aimed at ensuring that a more 'joined up' approach is taken to policy development and service delivery across central and local government departments, including closer links with the voluntary and independent sectors. This is both an acknowledgement of the extent of these difficulties and a welcome attempt to provide solutions. The changes to the management and organisation of youth justice services in particular have recognised the importance of achieving higher levels of co-ordination and planning between agencies.

Figure 2.1 illustrates the range of agencies involved in the processes of welfare and justice for children and young people, and the possible routes leading to placement into secure units. This figure demonstrates that there are a number of administrative and legal channels through which young people must pass before admission to a secure unit. At both central and local government levels there are different departments and agencies which have involvement in the decision-making processes that lead to young people being placed in a secure unit. Not all of these are criminal justice agencies. The Department of Health until recently had a management role in the now defunct Youth Treatment Service, and still has a critical role in the regulation, licensing and inspection of local authority secure units.

Characteristics of young people in secure accommodation

Antisocial Behaviour by Young People (Rutter *et al.* 1998) is a review of the literature and research about the nature of young people's antisocial behaviour, and the authors' conclusions afford an important overview of the current extent of our knowledge in this area. In addition they highlight the importance of studying trends over long periods of time and identifying the kinds of intervention likely to be most effective in the management and treatment of the different manifestations of antisocial behaviour. They summarise that antisocial behaviour is:

- Very common amongst young people, as British official statistics indicate that about a third of adult men will have a criminal record by the time they reach their mid-thirties, which in the main has been acquired as juveniles. Most delinquency is relatively minor, short-lived and theft-related. Serious and persistent offending is exhibited only by a small minority of young people, and only a small proportion of juvenile crime is violent.

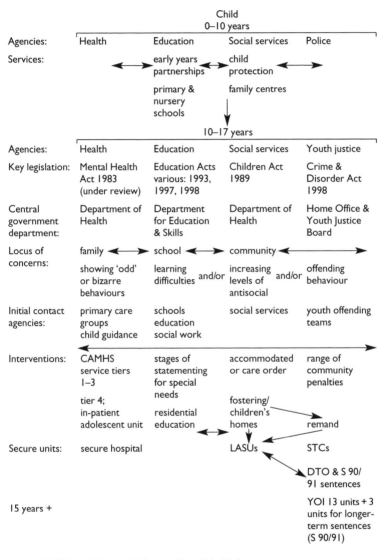

Note: CAMHS = Child and Adolescent Mental Health Service
       LASUs = local authority secure units
       S 90/91 = Sections 90 and 91 of the Powers of the Criminal Courts (Sentencing)
       Act 2000

Figure 2.1 Routes into secure accommodation

- Very varied in its manifestations so that it is meaningless to talk of, try to explain, or treat antisocial behaviour as if it was of only one 'type'. Consequently interventions need to be multi-modal and consistent over long periods of time, to be focused and targeted on criminogenic factors, to encourage pro-social behaviour, to involve and encourage families, to build on existing services, to be applied consistently and to combine different types of psycho-social treatments.
- Associated with a range of other problems including family characteristics, a history of disrupted or chaotic care, abuse and neglect, delinquent peer groups, school difficulties, and health problems, both physical and mental.

The varied nature of the behaviours makes it hard to identify significant groups of young people involved in antisocial behaviour for the purposes of intervention. However, Rutter *et al.* demonstrate that research would seem to indicate that the following factors are significant and have implications for planning intervention strategies:

- Early onset of antisocial behaviour associated with Attention Deficit Hyperactivity Disorder
- The age of onset, i.e. early or adolescent-specific
- Association with violence
- Psychopathy
- Mental disorder (linked to learning disability and substance abuse)

These conclusions are directly relevant to the planning of regimes and intervention strategies in secure units and offer a number of indicators which must be taken into account when designing regime provision and organising its delivery.

Rutter *et al.* also recognise that there is a good deal more work to be done in looking at the way in which differences of race and gender impact on the development of antisocial behaviour. Other researchers have commented on the way in which these factors also influence both sentencing and placement decisions. The policy commitment to remove all young women under the age of 18 years from prison service accommodation and place them in units in other parts of the secure estate comes at a time when the numbers of young women being sentenced to custody are increasing. This is another example of the ambivalence that besets this area of social policy. There is a consequent pressure to build new facilities for young women as well as to create space in other units that have the facilities to look after them. An unintended consequence of this, at least in the short term, is that more young men are likely to be placed in prison service establishments and further away from their own home communities than before. There is clearly some more analysis to be done about why the numbers of young women caught up in the criminal justice system are increasing, and in particular why custodial numbers are growing.

Similar concerns have been expressed over many years about the disproportionate numbers of young people from the minority black communities who are sentenced to custodial sentences, often at an earlier stage in their criminal careers than their white counterparts. Seventeen per cent of all male prisoners and 24 per cent of all female prisoners are from minority ethnic groups and these percentages are higher for young offenders (Morgan 1997). It is important not to tangle up the ways in which race and gender may be relevant to the origins and developmental patterns of antisocial behaviour in groups of children and young people with the ways in which different systems may define and respond to antisocial behaviour by young women and young black people, in terms of service delivery or sentencing and placement patterns. However, both are relevant for the practice of staff in secure units and the knowledge and skills that they must acquire in order to attend properly to the needs of young women and those from minority ethnic groups.

Common themes that emerge from almost all research studies about what factors influence antisocial behaviour in young people and involvement in the criminal justice system invariably include the following: family circumstances and, in particular, a history of offending by family members; low educational achievement; and mental health problems. A survey of young prisoners under the age of 21 found that as many as 38 per cent had experience of local authority care (National Prison Survey, Home Office 1991). This figure is even more startling when compared to the national average for the whole population which is only 2 per cent. This in itself demonstrates the general level of family disruption previously experienced by young people in custodial settings. Gwyneth Boswell in her research on the particular characteristics of young people who are sentenced to long-term imprisonment for grave crimes highlighted the high levels of specific trauma they had suffered. She found that in 200 cases studied only 18 young people had no reported experience of either some form of abuse or significant loss in their lives, and that 35 per cent of those interviewed had experienced both (Boswell 1995).

The report *Misspent Youth* (Audit Commission 1996) found that 42 per cent of school-age offenders sentenced in the Youth Court had been excluded from school, while another 23 per cent were persistent truants. Not only does prolonged time out of school affect educational achievement, but it also means long periods of time without constructive activity and increased opportunities to mix with similarly unmotivated young people and get involved in antisocial behaviour. In a comparative survey it was found that in the general population under 25 years old only 11 per cent had left school before the age of 16, but for male prisoners, 40 per cent had left school by this age (Home Office 1991).

The 1997 Office for National Statistics' survey of psychiatric morbidity amongst prisoners in England and Wales collected data about the particular circumstances of young prisoners aged 16–25 years. Their findings included the following:

- More than 6 out of 10 said that they had used some drug in the month before coming to prison. More than 70 per cent of the young offenders in all sample groups reported using at least one of the drugs considered in detail in this survey (cannabis, heroin, methadone, amphetamines, crack and cocaine powder) in the year before coming to prison.
- The most marked differences between male and female young offenders were in the receipt of mental health treatment. For example in the 12 months before entering prison, 11 per cent of sentenced and 13 per cent of remanded young male offenders had received help or treatment compared with 27 per cent of female young offenders.
- Among those who had a clinical interview, the prevalence of any personality disorder was 84 per cent for male remand and 88 per cent for male sentenced young offenders.
- The prevalence rates for any functional psychosis in the past year based on the clinical interview data were 10 per cent for male sentenced and 8 per cent for male remand young offenders.
- Women had generally higher CIS-R (Clinical Interview Schedule – Revised) scores than men in both remand and sentenced groups and were also more likely to suffer from a neurotic disorder. While 42 per cent of sentenced male young offenders in the sample had a CIS-R score of 12 or more the corresponding figure for women was 67 per cent.
- A larger proportion of respondents reported having suicidal thoughts .... The rates of suicide attempts were also high .... Women reported higher rates of suicidal thoughts and suicide

attempts than their male counterparts. For example, a third of the female sentenced respondents had tried to kill themselves in their lifetime, twice the proportion of male sentenced young offenders.

- The vast majority, over 96 per cent in all groups, had experienced at least one stressful life event and about two fifths had experienced five or more ....Women were far more likely than men to report having suffered as a result of violence at home and sexual abuse.

(Lader *et al.* 1997)

These overviews and research summaries provide us with a picture of young people in secure units that makes for salutary reading. On the whole the units are dealing with young people who are likely to have had disrupted and disturbed experiences of family life from a very early age, and many have been subject to various and often multiple forms of abuse by adults from whom they might have expected better. For a large number of these young people this has resulted in episodes of being in care, running away, and fractured links with any form of stable home life. A significant number of the young people have had difficulties at school with both teachers and other children. This has resulted later on in either exclusion or truancy, with the associated problems of having large amounts of unstructured time on their hands and contact with, or being influenced by, antisocial peer groups. A high number have experimented with various forms of drugs or alcohol, which in some cases means becoming dependent upon these substances. Many young people have longstanding mental health problems and there are a significant number who have Attention Deficit Disorder. A high percentage have attempted self-harm and/or had suicidal thoughts and many have attempted to act on these. Young people in secure units may present with one, some or all of these problems in any combination, with varying degrees of severity and differences in age of onset. There are also young people in secure units who have no such history and whose offence has been committed without any obvious antecedents or link to other known or associated factors. But what is clear is that by the time the overwhelming majority of young people come to secure units they have a personal history characterised by chaotic and disturbed developmental life experiences and relationships. Bringing some meaning and order to all this is a primary task for the secure setting.

Staff who work in secure units must be aware of the particular role that their unit plays within the whole range of services and agencies for children and young people, as well as having some understanding about how certain social factors may contribute to a young person's problems and what influence these may have had on their behaviour. Of course, most of the time staff in secure units do not need to think about this wider context or the way that systems operate. Their focus of attention has to be concentrated on the individual and groups of young people for whom they have responsibility and who are placed in their unit. It is the young people themselves who provide for the staff the primary source of the information that they need in order to look after them appropriately. It is in the context of ongoing daily care and activities that a young person begins to tell their story, sometimes in words and sometimes through their behaviour and actions. In the first instance, at least, staff do not get to understand the troubled and often troublesome young person with whom they are working by thinking about what their previous interactions with the various systems may reveal about their personality or needs. However, even at the individual level these are not mutually exclusive activities. Careful reflection often delivers up clues about how the experience of a young person through their sundry contacts with different systems and agencies has influenced present outcomes in terms of why they are where they are and why they are as they are.

A framework of ideas and knowledge about how social and psychological factors may contribute towards delinquent or disturbed behaviour in young people is essential. Only within that framework can an individual's experience and the unique content of their story be properly attended to and addressed. The one informs the other, but as we have seen, the demands and pressures of day-to-day work in a secure unit also require staff to have the resources to think about their immediate and confronting problems as they are experienced in dealings with the young people in the unit. It is to these ideas that we now turn.

Chapter 3

Ideas matter

'There is nothing either good or bad, but thinking makes it so.' Hamlet is talking with Rosencrantz and goes on to contrast their views of Denmark: 'To me it is a prison.' In making this remark Hamlet tells us something about his own current mental state and the way in which he is seeing the world. This power of thinking to make things seem either one way or another is given early recognition by Shakespeare who presumably didn't know much about cognitive behavioural therapies but did know a great deal about human nature and the way we experience the world around us.

In a television documentary about Feltham, the largest Young Offender Institution in England, a relative of a young person who had tragically hanged himself whilst on remand in the prison made a most telling comment in a very simple and moving way: 'Nobody thought about him.' This wasn't just a comment about busy staff who were under so much pressure because of the numbers of young people they had to 'process', although it was clear from the documentary that this was a feature of the institution's functioning. It was an insight into a system in which the demands on staff were not being managed in a way that recognised their need for time and space to think about an individual young person and through thinking to embark on a course of action that literally might have saved his life. Thinking 'hurts' because it means having to engage with the painful raw material that is generated in secure units when young people and adults come together. These are intense environments where, however strong the resistance and denial may be, there is no real escape from the conflict and pain that inevitably surface. This chapter is about that raw material and it suggests ways in which it might be thought about, which staff who work in secure units will, I hope, find useful.

An underlying assumption of this book is that past experiences affect the way individuals behave in the present, understand the world around them and shape their expectations as to how others are likely to behave towards them. As we have already noted, the life experiences of young people in secure accommodation are likely to have been at best unfortunate and in some instances profoundly damaging. This results in them having highly distorted views about their place in the world and in particular about the way adults are going to be able to look after them. It is a further assumption that although each adult member of staff brings their unique history into the setting they have achieved at least a certain maturity in their capacity to handle relationships and situations. Of course experience has shown that this is not always the case, and there have been a number of examples in residential care where adults have used their position of power and influence for their own perverse ends, although these have been mainly in open rather than secure settings. Despite this, adult members of staff who are involved on a daily basis in this work are on the whole making genuine and honest attempts to do their best in what can be very testing circumstances. What is true is that because of the intensity and the closeness of the relationships that develop between adults and young people in secure units each individual's history and current way of dealing with things tends to merge with the others. The result of this can be confusing for inexperienced staff who may find themselves carrying thoughts and feelings that they do not recognise as their own and are uncertain as to where they are coming from.

When a staff team is confident, well-supported and functioning cohesively, the outcome for young people is the experience of an adult group that is able to respond to them in ways that are affirming, nonjudgemental, consistent and fair. The adult group is consequently able to withstand the manifestations of the young people's disturbance, understand its origins and behave towards them in ways that challenge antisocial behaviours but encourage and reinforce each young person's positive aspects and qualities. To achieve this response from a staff group requires that they have at their disposal the necessary resources to fulfil their task, and that consistent and coherent systems of support are available to them. Making sure that these resources are accessible is an essential task for managers, who must also make sure that staff have access to what might be described as a tool box, which is kept full with ideas that they can use to develop their understanding, and also contains examples of the basic skills and techniques that they need to deal with what often seems like an inexhaustible range of difficult and disruptive behaviours.

Dealing with resistance to thinking

The compartment of the tool box that we are going to consider now is the one that holds the ideas that are needed for understanding what can appear to be the muddle of events and activities that go on inside secure units. This is the right place to start because unless staff have some understanding about what is going on around them it is unlikely that their responses and behaviour will be effective in managing or changing a young person's behaviour or helping them to think about things differently. It is this process of thinking and understanding which often seems to be so difficult to achieve. Partly this is because organisational demands put staff groups under pressure but also because there is always some resistance on the part of the staff and young people's groups to engage in the process. Although the ways in which their resistance works are different, they share a common underlying reason. This is probably best described as intense anxiety about the feelings that might be stirred up if the horrifying detail about what has happened to the young people is confronted.

Anxiety may be defined as a response to an inner affect or thought that is frightening because of the consequence, real or imagined, that would ensue if the individual acted upon the affect or thought. For the young people in secure accommodation the difficulties they have experienced over many years often lie buried too deep for words. They simply do not have the emotional vocabulary to talk about what has happened to them. It often seems much better to try to run away – which, in many cases, has literally been the young person's previous reaction before placement – or to fight against what they perceive to be attempts to make them think about these deeply painful issues. Placement in a secure unit can have a positive effect by challenging both responses, and staff and young people often recognise that to have the opportunity of being in one place for a period of time is of therapeutic benefit, especially if the time also includes opportunities for thinking and reflection.

As Murray Cox comments: 'One of the consequences of anxiety is that it diminishes horizons, intensifies tunnel vision and reduces possibility' (Cox 1998: 219). In residential settings the avoidance of professional supervision, which is designed to focus on supporting and developing staff in their work, is a common problem. Even when supervision of this type is available at a reasonable level there are always 'good' reasons why it can't happen today! In prison service establishments for young people under 18 years there is no model of staff supervision for prison officers in this sense at all. In the same way how many staff meetings spend interminable hours discussing matters that could very easily be resolved outside a meeting? On one occasion in a residential unit the whole of a weekly staff meeting was spent in a detailed and heated discussion about how the toothpaste for the young people was best distributed. Now it could be that there is a clever interpretation about what toothpaste might represent to a stressed staff group, but in this case there is a more likely and simple explanation. This was a poorly managed group of staff working together in a unit that was barely functioning. The agenda could have been explosive but in the staff meeting the manager colluded with the staff's avoidance of what would have been a painful discussion of some difficult issues. After the meeting everyone was relieved at some level that toothpaste had dominated proceedings, but on the other hand there was undoubtedly a good deal of frustration that nothing much had seemed to happen or been resolved.

Young people have their own ways of preventing thinking. Their very presence on a unit means that not all the staff at any one time can attend a meeting. Alarm bells seem to go off regularly in staff-meeting time or when staff are gathering to hand over from one shift to another. These occasions in residential units when staff meet are the focus of intense attention from young people. Partly this is because they know that these are opportunities for decisions to be made by the adult group about certain aspects of their programme – for example, any change in their status on the incentive scheme. But there are perhaps some more deep-seated feelings that are evoked by these occasions – the whispering of adults in another room, a sense of being excluded, a fear of who might come from or into the locked room and what the consequences of that might be. There is also a great fear that their personal and individual 'business', as they call it, will be shared. The closed staff-room door is an object of real feeling for young people and often of real attack! Preventing staff from getting together and thinking also carries some ambivalence for young people. For despite their protestations there is a sense in which to be the focus of the adults' attention and time is what they want above all else. The competition that exists amongst young people within these sorts of residential groups is often extraordinarily fierce, and more than anything it is competition for staff time. Attacks on thinking time are intended to prevent things happening, but they are also about claiming something as well, i.e. attention, but always on an individual basis as most of these young people are too damaged to have much of a sense of group need. In order to make some more sense of this the model in Figure 3.1 may be considered.

As the model illustrates, it is the continuous intermingling of daily routines, programme events and unpredictable incidents that provides the

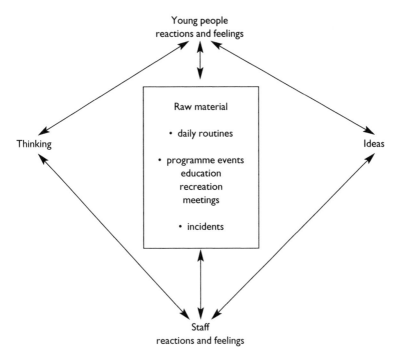

Figure 3.1

raw material to which staff and young people contribute but to which they are also required to respond and react. From the staff point of view, to make their responses helpful they have to have understanding, but, as we shall see, it is also part of the staff team's purpose to encourage the young people to share in this reflective activity and so begin to increase their understanding. For young people to learn to think and behave differently rather than just repeating earlier antisocial behaviour is a fundamental aim of the whole process.

The ideas we are now going to explore in some detail are taken from a range of different theoretical perspectives and clinical applications. It is often these applications that determine the way in which these concepts are defined, and their use often varies depending upon the setting in which they are applied. Our setting is the residential secure unit and our starting point is the nature of the relationships that are formed by the groups of adult staff and young people through their mutual sharing in the routines of daily life and the interactions that arise from them.

The meaning of containment

Containment is a term often used to portray a rather limited process almost synonymous with the act of locking up. In its psychological application, however, it is the term that may be used to describe the fundamental task that we have described above, in which staff 'hold on to' material presented by the young people, process it and give it back in a way that is more manageable and understandable. In a secure unit this containment is derived primarily from the activity of the staff but also from the design and nature of the building itself in the way that it provides security and safety. This is why it is so disheartening to staff when the building is seen to fail as a result of damage caused to it by the young people, or when design and maintenance faults allow the possibility of a young person being able to hurt themselves. Albeit in different roles, I have over the years been fortunate enough, or perhaps some might say unfortunate enough, to have been involved in the early developmental stages of three important residential units for young people. Two of these facilities had secure units as part of their overall provision and one was a therapeutic unit for older adolescents in open conditions. All three are still operational and successful in their own right. On each occasion the initial problems were very similar, although the ways of managing and resolving them varied. Each development included a substantial building project, a significant financial, administrative and personnel function, and a huge investment in staff recruitment with an allied programme of induction and continuing training. Even with all this ongoing and necessary activity, however, the most important dimension remained the clear articulation of the purpose of each unit and the setting out, to use a much overworked word, of the vision on which they were founded. Interestingly the three projects were developed using practice models that drew upon different traditions. The focus of one was on using behavioural theories to inform interventions, with a strong token economy system as the main vehicle for shaping the relationships between staff and young people. Another drew much more upon the traditions of therapeutic communities, whilst the third was based on developing a model in which different interventions, including cognitive behavioural techniques, were employed with individual and groups of young people within an agreed framework of psychodynamic thinking about child development, the functioning of groups and the nature and meaning of relationships within a therapeutic setting. Almost irrespective, however, of the particular model used for the development of the residential unit, each situation required a clear set of ideas with which newly recruited

staff could identify in a way that caught their imagination and commitment. This was not something that just happened, although in each case
there needed to be enough flexibility in the process to take account of the
particular and emerging dynamics within the staff groups and use the
individual skills of members of staff as these became known and obvious.
This process is described as follows in an article written about one of the
units shortly after its opening.

> Critical to the success of the induction process was the recognition
> that the newly formed groups of staff had to be given an authentic
> role in shaping and forming an organisation whose core purpose is to
> care for some of the most disordered young people in the country. It
> was not good enough just to talk about therapeutic work, the initial
> experiences of the new staff, the induction programme and the writ-
> ing and agreement of policy and practice procedures had to reflect
> the processes that are integral to therapeutic work. The induction
> programme took place over three months and included a combin-
> ation of formal training sessions, 'experiential' sessions and the
> creation of a daily routine that replicated as far as possible the group
> nature of residential work. Within a given framework of values and
> core principles the staff team was encouraged to take responsibility
> for developing a wide ranging policy and practice framework that
> still directly affects the quality of daily life and work .... This frame-
> work was embodied in a mission statement which was often referred
> to throughout the induction programme when worries arose about
> the likely realities of working with the young people.
>
> (J. Rose 1998)

It is worth noting that the mission statement referred to was the product
of a two-day workshop involving managers at all levels in the organisation who made their individual contributions to the final agreed
statement.

As the three residential establishments became operational, similar
problems emerged in each. These included inconsistencies arising from
lack of known routines; confusion over roles and responsibilities; incon-
sistent responses to difficult behaviour from the young people; serious
bullying amongst the young people; the inevitable testing out of both
human and mechanical systems by the young people who themselves felt
uncertain in a shifting and changing environment; and an over-reliance
on managers to provide instant solutions for both the staff and young
people. All of these resulted in a rapid yo-yoing of staff morale and

months of what seemed like chaos as staff and young people grappled with what sometimes felt a frightening environment in which to work or live. The key element in moving on from this to a situation in which some order was established and in which it became possible to describe a culture for the organisation was a growing sense of containment. Again this did not just happen; there are no easy answers in this work and certainly no magical solutions. Progress was made through the sheer persistent efforts of staff in delivering the core tasks of the daily routine and in ensuring that planned programme activities were provided in an increasingly consistent and reliable way. As this was happening, the staff teams became more confident and more able to use their given opportunities for talking and reflecting. Over a period of time, and through shared activities, the staff's relationships with the young people in their care were strengthened as everyone began to feel more secure and safer in their surroundings. The model in Figure 3.2 illustrates the processes involved.

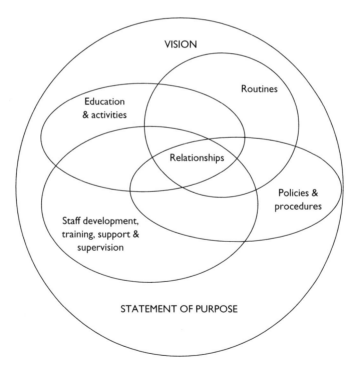

Figure 3.2

Providing this sort of containment is important not just at an organisational or group level but also for the safe care and management of individuals. Another way of understanding containment is to think about it as the ability to tolerate intense negative feelings without acting on them. To get to this point is the task of a staff group not only for themselves but more importantly for each young person. As we have seen before, this means creating opportunities in which young people are encouraged to do some thinking and talking about their lives for themselves. This is not a quick-fix approach and the work will not necessarily be completed whilst a young person is in a secure unit. Average lengths of stay in all forms of secure accommodation are generally of a short duration, often a matter of three months or less. As much as staff might want to get into some of the detail of this kind of work it is not wise to expect to do so. Even where a young person is spending a longer period of time in a secure unit much of the work likely to be done is probably better thought of as preparation for future therapeutic work. However, this does not negate the importance of creating a containing environment which is safe for both staff and young people and in which staff are aware of what is going on for a young person whilst endeavouring to achieve more stable behaviour. At this time, as so often in work with young people, it may be mainly the staff group or a member of staff who has to do the thinking on behalf of the young person and be the one who begins to find the right words to express the feelings behind the behaviours.

> The levels of containment that prisons and hospitals provide are important as for some individuals they provide a concrete substitute sense of ego (and also super-ego) a form of second skin, where boundlessness and boundaries come together.
>
> (Delshadian 2001)

The meaning of behaviour

A good deal of staff time in secure units seems to be spent chasing from one crisis to another or just simply keeping the wheels turning. At the same time as doing all of this the difficult and disruptive behaviour of the young people has to be managed. Amidst the pressures of daily life the definition of this behaviour or the reaction to it sometimes does not go much further than to classify it as bad and to dismiss the young person as a pain in the proverbial! Now in a practical sense, in the context of a secure unit with a group of young people, there has to be some action on behalf of staff to manage disruptive and potentially dangerous behaviour.

Staff have to be confident to intervene and have at their disposal a range of techniques to use in different circumstances. They also need to know, however, what it is that they are dealing with when they do so. This knowledge comes out of a process of staff discussion and learning about each young person, and a certain amount of 'trial and error' in the application of different management methods. In the kind of situations that so easily and quickly develop in a secure unit it may be that actions have to precede words, but they should never precede thought. Acting intuitively only gets you so far. The psychoanalyst Wilfred Bion used a most telling phrase when writing about his work during the second world war and in particular his involvement in developing techniques for training officers in the army. He called it the ability to 'think under fire', or in other words whilst in the heat of battle retaining the capacity to think in the here and now rather than just with hindsight (Young 1995). It is the extent of a staff team's capacity to think about a group of young people and to anticipate their needs and likely responses to situations that differentiates a mature team from an immature one.

The ideas tool box can be raided here by taking the assumption that all behaviour has a meaning and then going on to try to answer the question, what does this particular piece of behaviour tell us? In seeking the answer to this question it is helpful to think about the concept of defence and defence mechanisms.

The nature of defences

Most of us have some idea about the nature and meaning of defences and the different ways in which the term can be used. In football, for example, we readily acknowledge defending as an essential part of the game with the purpose of protecting and resisting attacks on goal. Many pundits argue that without a strong defence there can be no meaningful play and that a weak defence ultimately reduces to failure attempts to fashion a winning team. We also have some idea about the importance of a national defence policy and the need for a strong defence to protect against or to warn off potential aggressors from an attack which might threaten our very existence. These notions all apply when thinking about the meaning of defences in a more psychological way, as mechanisms by means of which impulses, feelings and fantasies are kept from conscious awareness or from action in order to avoid the anxiety associated with them. We all employ such mechanisms as part of our daily lives, often as ways of coping with those particular situations we find most stressful. Some of the most common defences are immediately recognisable from ordinary life, such as the very young child who when confronted with some obvious misdemeanour spontaneously says, 'it wasn't me'. This denial is often maintained in the light of incontestable evidence, not least from a frustrated adult who replies, 'but I saw you do it!' Similarly, when a child places their hands over their eyes and apparently becomes convinced at that moment that they cannot be seen and cease to exist in the objective world, the understanding of this particular form of defence mechanism is quite straightforward. Most of us are able to identify with the person who after a busy day at work and another harrowing interview with the boss, in which their brilliance has yet again gone unrecognised, returns home and takes out their feelings by throwing a slipper at the poor cat. Calling this displacement and analysing it as a psychological defence mechanism might be plausible but probably not instantly welcome, certainly not by the cat! In the same sort of way the idea of splitting may be explored through a general consideration of how in families children will come up with a phrase like, 'dad lets me do it, why won't you?' These are trivial and rather inconsequential examples of what are really some quite complicated psychological processes. However, anyone with any experience of spending time with young people who have problems of the severity experienced by those who are placed in secure units will immediately be able to recognise the processes described and think of their own examples.

Projection

Another very familiar defence mechanism which will be recognised by those working with damaged people is projection. This is when an individual takes the often unacceptable characteristics or features of themselves and locates them in another person, usually roundly condemning them for what is in effect their own difficulty or failing. This can leave an unsuspecting worker carrying some very odd feelings, the origins of which they are uncertain about and yet with which they uncannily seem to identify. In how many staff meetings do the staff team find quite opposing views about an individual young person being put forward? Often these discussions provoke a great deal of feeling on both sides. Individual members of staff commonly find themselves the particular target of a young person's verbal or physical abuse directed personally towards them. In a lot of settings one of two things might happen by way of response. The staff team may recognise what is going on, at least at the behavioural level, and come up with a strategy to protect the member of staff. This usually involves some punishment of the young person, but no effort is made to understand the behaviour. In the worst case other members of the team heave a sigh of relief that they are not the one under fire and leave the member of staff to suffer alone, probably resulting in their increasing disillusionment with the job, a feeling of deep failure and in the most extreme situations eventual resignation.

In both cases some use of the idea of defence could be helpful. In the first instance, thinking about the splitting in the staff team might lead to some thoughts about the young person and what is represented by the two sides of their presentation. In the first place it is important to have a regular arrangement for properly managed team meetings in which these sorts of ideas can be thoroughly discussed and followed through over a period of time rather than just being the topic in a one-off meeting. Unless time is taken to really look at the presenting behaviour of a young person and to think through what their behaviour might mean then the likelihood is that decisions taken will be solely reactive and influenced by whatever pressures are most immediate and strongest. The most vocal or most anxious of staff can easily hold sway when these sorts of discussions are being held.

In the second example, whilst it is very important for the team as a whole to send out the message that the targeting of staff is unacceptable and will not be tolerated, it is almost certainly likely to be the case that the member of staff involved is the object of some projection by the young person. Again the forum of a supportive staff meeting can be used to create some safe opportunity to explore what is going on, and can prove to be of great benefit to both of them.

Acting out

It is said that the best form of defence is attack or, to put it another way, get your retaliation in first. This is another familiar experience to those who work with troubled young people. Many of the young people in secure units have had deeply disturbing experiences of adults, and rather than run the risk of being hurt again often attack first. This attacking behaviour is referred to as 'acting out' and is literally a way of behaving in the external world to either block out or prevent having to think about what is going on so painfully inside the mind. Rather than talk about what is going on, young people may either be hostile and aggressive to others or turn the feelings inwards and try to harm themselves. This latter behaviour can sometimes be an example of displacement, by which a young person attacks their own body rather than directing their feelings towards the one with whom they are truly angry.

Acting out takes different forms and is not just about bad behaviour. It may have some more subtle manifestations but these serve the same purpose. An example of this is the young person whose behaviour and attitudes align them more with the staff group than their peers. In appearing mature, perhaps by taking responsibility for an aspect of unit life, a young person becomes more like a member of staff than the average member of the staff team. John was a young person who shortly after being admitted to the secure unit volunteered to become the unit librarian. Not only did he catalogue everything perfectly and issue tickets efficiently, he even dressed the part in suit and tie, carrying a briefcase to 'work' every day. He was never a management problem and would engage in long discussions with staff about what was going on in the unit and offer his views about how things could be made significantly better for everyone. It was sometimes hard to remember why John was in the unit and various staff expressed the view that it was a pity he was there. In fact John had killed his girlfriend's sister and then hidden her body in a very well-planned, cold and calculated manner. I am not sure that we really took his behaviour as acting out and we were probably glad that he gave us no problems in the unit. It is only now, many years on, that I can begin to think about what might have been going on, whereas some advice or challenge at the time to us as a staff team about what we were doing in our collusion would have been good.

Self-harm

Looking after a young person or a group of young people who self-harm is one of the most stressful aspects of this work in any setting. Coming to work in the morning uncertain as to whether or not a young person has survived the night is a chilling experience for a member of staff, particularly if it involves someone with whom they have a close relationship. Within a secure unit there is at least more likelihood of being able to manage the environment and prevent objects that can be used for self-harming from being readily available. However, this does not prevent a young person who is determined to behave in this way from seeking out opportunities and making the attempt. In trying to prevent self-harm, staff may become over-concerned with the behaviours and lose sight of the fact that they need to understand the meaning behind them. The behaviour is only a symptom of something more profound which needs to be explored.

Staff reactions to self-harm vary and there is a strong individual component to them. It is important that staff are able to share their feelings about self-harm as it manifests in individual young people and to understand their feelings in relation to each individual young person. It is important too that staff, both individually and in teams, are able to respond to episodes of self-harm rather than just react, and therefore become able to engage with the young person at more than just a superficial level through managing the behaviour. If possible the responsibility for managing self-harm should be a shared one amongst the whole group, including the young people. It is not possible to engage with the problem of this kind of acting out if it is approached as just an issue for the individual. Questions have to be asked about the relationships within the young people's group, and it is also worthwhile exploring the different reactions which are located in the adult staff group. The weight of the feelings that this behaviour places upon the adult group needs to be a shared burden and is more tolerable if taken on by the adult group as a whole. As with other aspects of the process we have described for working with young people, the adult group have the responsibility to hold the material with which they are presented, but at the same time must find ways of passing it back to the young people so that they can develop understanding and also take responsibility for changing the ways in which they cope with their distress and pain. Both as individuals and as a group, young people have to learn to help themselves.

There are different models for understanding self-harm and also for its management. It is critical that each unit has a model which is known and understood by all staff, and that staff are familiar with the procedures that are in place to deal with situations as they occur. It is important that managers are able to support staff when these procedures have been followed, and are prepared to manage the anxieties that such incidents provoke in those outside the residential unit. One of the most destructive elements of self-harm is the way in which blame becomes a standard response to incidents, and it is essential that managers do not foster this in the way that they approach staff when reflecting on such an episode.

Case study

Most of us employ a number of psychological defences to help us order our daily lives, but for the young people we are concerned to help something else has happened. The defence has taken over and assumed a significance in the way that they relate to people and manage situations, a way that is largely dysfunctional – understandable maybe, but dysfunctional. This is partly because the anxiety being avoided is so great. In the

following case study we can see how Ben's behaviour incorporated a number of defence mechanisms which caused
enormous problems in his relationships with others but also
almost entirely crippled his ability to live a normal daily life.
He was a young person who created great anxiety in the staff
team looking after him, partly because of his violent outbursts
but also because of the extreme and constant demands he
made on their emotional and physical energies.

Ben was 15 years old at the time of his admission to the unit.
He was admitted from a mental health adolescent unit from
which he had been excluded as a result of his part in a serious
sexual assault on a young female patient. Ben's father had left
the home and his mother before Ben was born and there had
subsequently been very little contact between him and Ben.
Dad in fact only returned to the family home some fourteen
years later after Ben had moved into care, spending just
enough time to impregnate Ben's mother which resulted, from
Ben's point of view at least, in an unwanted baby sister. Much
of Ben's early upbringing was shared between his mother and
maternal grandmother, an alcoholic woman who, according to
information available, continually and persistently denigrated
and abused her daughter. The reason for social services becoming involved with the family was that Ben's mother com-
plained that he was becoming increasingly violent and abusive
towards her. This had apparently increased from around the
age of 12, although she described him as always having been a
difficult child to look after. There had been several violent
attacks by Ben on his mother and she had required hospital
treatment on more than one occasion. Ben's mother was
extremely ambivalent about her relationship with her son, and
over the period of his stay in the unit never gave any explicit
message about whether or not she would maintain contact
with him or have him live at home again. This latter possibility
was Ben's dominating motivation and hope for the future.

Ben's presenting difficulty was his highly obsessive behaviour. He would repeat the same question endlessly throughout
the day, pursuing a thought or an idea without a break. He
performed a number of rituals continuously: touching his head

to make sure every hair was in place, touching his shoes, avoiding walking on any cracked paving stone. He was always running late during the morning's activities, often not appearing from his room until lunch time, as before he could leave his bedroom he had to complete a number of routines, mainly to do with his own personal hygiene and the cleanliness of his room. At night he could be heard completing a similar set of routines before settling to sleep which was always preceded by three turns of the bedroom door handle.

Despite his own obvious difficulties Ben was quick to point out the deficiencies of others, especially where this was to do with their poor hygiene, lack of educational ability or some imagined sexual perversion. He had unrealistic ambitions concerning the likelihood of his own educational success, but he was a bright boy and on occasions could show some insight into his circumstances and difficulties. Ben's criticism of other young people was couched in the cruellest and crudest of language liberally sprinkled with rich and explicit sexual insults. On occasions he was very violent towards members of the staff group, particularly female staff, often appearing to treat the adults as though they were objects for his own use.

Ben's behaviour was problematic for the residential group. The nature and level of his violence required careful monitoring and management approaches. Staff were often wary of engaging with him, not just because of the violence which was actually sporadic but because the manner of his relating to people was utterly demanding and exhausting. There were clearly many facets to Ben's behaviour and the staff team spent a lot of time trying to think about and understand his extremely disturbing day-to-day presentation. The concept of defences was helpful for understanding the compulsive, obsessive dimensions of his behaviour and in particular the idea of reaction formation. This describes a mechanism of defence in which a drive, feeling or idea is countered by a drive, feeling or idea opposite in quality. A reaction formation may become fixed and stable and form an important part of an individual's character structure. In Ben's case the obsessive need for order and cleanliness in his external world, coupled with his own unrealistic desires for achievement, might be thought about as a way of defending against the chaos and mess of his internal world and the enormously angry feelings that he had. The highly sexualised content of much of the abuse he directed towards others would be another example of his anxiety about his own sexuality. Certainly he could proffer no worse insult than to label someone 'queer'. We speculated a good deal about whether or not he had been sexually abused at any stage, but there was no evidence for this. Ben's relationship with his mother was intense, and after being together with them staff felt uncomfortable and spoke of sensing a sexual charge between them. Of course, as with so many of these most troubled young people, even the most well-rehearsed defences could not contain the underlying feelings and from time to time they were acted out in a destructive and violent fashion. These occasions did become fewer over a long period of time as Ben slowly began to experience a different type of containment, although in the longer term the prognosis remained poor.

Managing defensive behaviours

One of the most difficult aspects of working with young people is being able to distinguish between what might be considered normal adolescent behaviour and behaviour which is actually an expression of disturbance. A complicating factor is that the behaviours may be both things at the same time. In the example of John, the young librarian, there clearly were dimensions of his behaviour that were positive and which the staff rightly supported and worked to strengthen. The psychological defence he was actually employing is called sublimation, in which there is a displacement of a basic or instinctual aim in an apparent conformity with higher societal values. It is the most advanced and mature of defence mechanisms as it allows partial expression of conscious drives in a modified, socially acceptable and desirable way. Disturbed young people often make strenuous attempts to adopt behaviours that mimic the more effective coping styles of their less disturbed and more emotionally mature peers. To describe this process, Donald Winnicott wrote about the 'false self' which a young person constructs in an attempt to convince themselves, and others, that their internal world is more integrated and stable than is really the case (Winnicott 1956). While it is encouraging to see and to respond to such apparently positive elements in the lives of these young people, it is critical to properly assess the function that these behaviours serve. Without this analysis it may be that interventions aimed at strengthening positive aspects of young people's lives will inadvertently serve to reinforce defensive rather than coping strategies. The complexity of all this shows that while challenging and confronting defensive behaviour is an important part of the staff task it needs to be done sensitively and in the context of a relationship in which there is genuine value and regard for the other. It is also why it is so important to have a sound grasp of the principles of child development. Understanding the significance of the different developmental milestones, and in particular having a grasp of the processes occurring in the stage of development called adolescence, is essential for staff working in secure units. Only by having a clear grasp of how children grow up in 'normal' circumstances is it possible to begin to understand some of the damaging effects that particular experiences have on this process and the potential consequences of these in later life.

The meaning of attachment

Thinking about early attachment experiences as an important factor in the way a person is able to form relationships and behave towards others in later life has been a current focus in much recent research. The British psychoanalyst, John Bowlby, was among the first to focus on the importance of an infant's need for an unbroken (secure) early attachment to the mother. He later suggested that disruption in the functioning of the attachment system is likely to interfere with a child's developing capacity for regulating their behaviour, emotions and arousal (Bowlby 1973). In a most useful and informative book, Howe and colleagues provide a comprehensive and detailed exploration of the importance of early attachments and the possible consequences in later life if the quality of these is impaired.

> The quality and character of children's close relationships is proving to be the central concept linking the myriad of factors that have a bearing upon development.
>
> (Howe *et al.* 1999: 9)

A child's development is dependent upon the way in which a number of key factors relate to each other and are integrated by the child into their growing awareness of the world around them. These factors are a combination of social and inter-personal phenomena.

> Increasingly, it is being recognised that, psychologically, the individual cannot be understood independently of his or her social and cultural context. The infant does not enter the world as an *a priori* discrete psychological being. Rather, the self and personality form as the developing mind engages with the world in which it finds itself. There is thus no hard boundary between the mental condition of individuals and the social environments in which they find themselves.
>
> (ibid.: 9)

Howe goes on to describe different types of attachment experience and to illustrate how these different early experiences of children in relation to their primary care figures influence their behavioural responses and subsequent patterns of responding to situations and relationships. Useful examples are given showing the different kinds of behavioural responses that may appear later on as a result of some kind of poor early attachment experience and how these can affect important areas of life, particularly in the making and sustaining of relationships.

A further important aspect of this research seeks to connect the detail of early attachment experiences to later antisocial or delinquent behaviour. Peter Fonagy has provided an interesting overview of a number of research findings which explore and demonstrate the links between attachment experiences and later offending and antisocial behaviours, in particular those associated with acts of violence (Fonagy and Target 1998). Although there can be no straightforward assumptions about a linear continuity, 'attachment research has demonstrated that there are marked continuities in children's security of attachment, maintained probably by the stable quality of the parent–child relationship' (ibid.: 138). Thinking about the varying attachment experiences for children and their possible relationship to different sorts of later antisocial behaviours is an important area of study.

For staff engaged in day-to-day work with young people who have been placed in secure units, using the ideas of attachment theory provides an interesting way to reflect upon the meaning of current presenting behaviour from young people and to try to link this with the immediate circumstances that have led to their placement in secure accommodation, as well as with their earlier formative experiences where these are known. Such reflection may also provide important clues not just about why a young person is behaving in a particular way but about why certain approaches that might be used to establish a relationship are more or less successful. Staff are often puzzled as to why some young people do not appear to respond to their well-intentioned and genuinely offered approaches of support. In fact the experience is often one of strong rejection, which can be dispiriting and puzzling to new staff who cannot understand why their best efforts seem to be thrown back in their face by the young people they are trying to help. Being able to depersonalise this rejection, and to see it in the context of how a young person may themselves have been consistently rejected or never had an opportunity to make a good or lasting relationship, is an important learning point. In a similar way, difficulties between individual members of staff and a young person are often put down to differences in personality, but in every unit there will have been the experience of a young person who appears to be too much for whole staff teams and whom no one seems able to engage. The response to these young people is usually to move them on to another unit in the hope that somewhere they will find someone with whom they can make a relationship. Thinking in these instances about the nature of the young person's earlier attachments may be a useful way forward in planning for longer-term management and treatment, allowing more realistic goals to be set and not creating impossible expectations which the young person will never be able to fulfil.

The power of transference

Staff in secure units are mostly confined to working with the young people in their care in the here and now events and activities of the daily routine. Group meetings or discussion invariably focus on immediate issues, although it is quite probable that discussions with young people will also include the circumstances that have resulted in placement in a secure unit, and part of the staff's task is to make links between a young person's behaviour prior to admission and their behaviour inside the unit. What is less likely to be touched upon are a young person's earlier experiences and how these have shaped their present attitudes and behaviour. The model in Figure 3.3 illustrates how these different areas of experience, although distanced by periods of time, may be understood and related to each other.

In talking with groups of residential staff, however, it is not necessary to spend too long or use advanced psychotherapeutic techniques for the conversation to get around to what it feels like to do this sort of work. and in particular how the young people make them feel. I have heard a num-

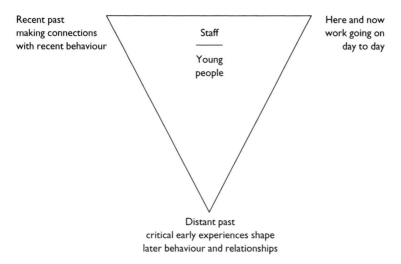

Recent past
making connections
with recent behaviour

Staff
———
Young
people

Here and now
work going on
day to day

Distant past
critical early experiences shape
later behaviour and relationships

Figure 3.3

ber of prison officers who have been in the prison service for many years, but with limited experience of working with the younger population, say things like, 'this is the first time I have ever gone home and dreamed about a prisoner'. A group of experienced residential staff working in a secure unit were asked to list what they thought the young people they worked with were like. The list was lengthy and included: delinquent, damaged, disturbed, stroppy, materialistic, frightened, manipulative, difficult, frustrated, always right, insecure, lonely, suspicious, angry, not able to communicate, out of control, violent, good liars, hurting, smart, depressed, suicidal, needy, chaotic. The same group of staff were then asked how the young people they worked with made them feel. It was interesting to note how similar the lists looked when they were put together. The strength of the feelings behind some of the descriptions given of the young people mirrored closely the feelings experienced by the staff in their daily contact with them. We have previously identified the process of projection, whereby one person puts out their bad feelings into another, but there is another set of processes which it is important for staff to be able to think about, which involves what is known as transference and counter-transference. The prison officer who took home his work with a young person and dreamed about it was clearly involved in an intense relationship. This wasn't something he particularly sought or necessarily encouraged. The young person 'got under his skin' in a way that these young people do when they re-enact through members of staff earlier experiences and relationships. Greenson has defined transference as:

> The experiencing of feelings, drives, attitudes, fantasies and defences toward a person in the present, which do not befit that person but are a repetition of reactions originating in regard to significant persons of early childhood, unconsciously displaced onto figures in the present. The two outstanding characteristics of a transference reaction are: it is a repetition and it is inappropriate.
>
> (Greenson 1967: 155)

In formal psychotherapeutic settings counter-transference is the term used to describe the thoughts and feelings experienced by the therapist in their work with a patient. At one stage these were regarded as obstacles that could easily get in the way of understanding the problems of the patient. Over time, however, it has become axiomatic that the thoughts and feelings of the therapist are a tool to be used in the therapeutic process and can provide important indicators about the condition of the patient through examination of the effect they are having upon the therapist. As well as sometimes being confused about the strength and nature of their own feelings, staff are often amazed at the way in which the young people seem to know things about them or their colleagues or are able to tune into the mood of a member of staff or even the whole staff group. Experience shows that often it is the most disturbed of all young people who seem to have the greatest capacity for this kind of unconscious communication.

In individual or group psychotherapy a central focus of the work is to explore the nature and meaning of transference relationships. In the setting of secure units and in the day-to-day work of the staff group transference is important more as a reference for staff when trying to disentangle and make sense of the bewildering complexity of feelings and emotions that run continuously through the unit. Transference is also important in helping to provide some understanding of why relationships with the young people feel so intense. Reducing the frequency of what is often called staff 'burn out' might be helped by a greater understanding in these settings of the effect of transference in relationships with disturbed people. It is interesting to note that in the case of Ben, discussed previously, his female key worker finally acknowledged that the real reason she was leaving the unit was not the promotion that she had gained but to get away from Ben. Such honesty is rare because the impact of the young people on the psychological health of staff is not readily acknowledged as a source of staff stress. Nevertheless, having talked with a good number of residential staff, I am sure that it figures high on the list of reasons for many people leaving residential work and seeking employment in alternative settings. The fact that this can happen is also an indictment of the inadequate levels of supervision and support provided by the majority of institutions, in which the powerful influence of these processes is barely recognised.

However, it must be remembered that staff in secure units are not employed as, or expected to be, psychotherapists. That is a specialist role and there are very few psychotherapists working in secure units. The work of staff, who provide much of the day-to-day care for the young people in secure units, is to engage with them in the here and now activities of daily life and to provide as positive a group experience and as much individual support as they can. Most of what gets talked about relates to the immediate experience of life in the unit and most of the behaviours that are challenged are ones that are displayed in interactions between young people and staff on the unit. The quality of the experience for young people placed in secure units is determined largely by the quality of their relationships with staff and other young people in the daily life of the unit. This critical role of staff is also likely to be highly determinate in any evaluation of the outcomes of the period of time spent by a young person in a unit. Life in secure units can be a bit like living in the fast lane. This is why creating definite spaces for thinking and reflection is important not just for the staff group but for the young people as well. It is in those moments that drawing upon the ideas sketched out in this chapter may provide some useful ways of furthering understanding and informing strategies in practice.

A corrective emotional experience

To talk about a secure unit as providing a corrective emotional experience for young people may appear to be rather old-fashioned. In fact it describes the overall task very well and links back to the idea in the introduction about the importance of a young person encountering a culture in the secure unit that offers a different kind of experience of what relationships with adults can actually mean.

A corrective emotional experience involves an exposure under more favourable circumstances to situations that an individual could not handle in the past. In order to be helped, that individual must undergo a corrective emotional experience suitable to repair the traumatic influence of previous experiences. For change to occur, the experience must have both an emotional and a corrective element. Applied to a secure setting, the environment must provide each young person with a significantly different kind of experience of adult care and authority that is both warm and has a genuine emotional content. As well, however, there has to be a cognitive element to the process which allows experiences to be reflected upon and talked about so that new learning can take place to address problems and change previous patterns of behaviour. This neatly begins to suggest a way of bringing together the different aspects of work in secure units, in which attention has to be given to the nature of the overall experience for the young person in terms of daily group life and its associated relationships, and the kind of individual or formal group work that is required to stimulate the processes of thinking and change.

'Life can only be understood backwards; but it must be lived forwards', wrote the Danish philosopher Sören Kierkegaard. For adolescents, the process of transition from childhood to adulthood brings together the past, present and future more intensely than at any other stage of life. Adults who are involved in providing care for some of the most damaged young people need to understand something about each young person's past and help them to look with hope towards the future. To do this requires making a number of important connections: between the past and the present, between the internal and external worlds of individuals, groups and organisations, and in the myriad of complex relationships that go to make up the world of secure units. Thinking about this may be hard but it is worthwhile and essential if there is to be any real move from chaos to culture.

Chapter 4

It's the stories that are important

Life in a secure unit may be considered from a number of different perspectives but these must include the particular and individual stories of the adults and young people who work and live there. These accounts, if taken seriously, inform the development of ideas about effective practice and management in a particularly powerful way. The voices of residential staff and young people both tend to get lost in the general hubbub that passes for debate about the role and purpose of secure accommodation for young people.

In this chapter we look at a piece of research undertaken by the Trust for the Study of Adolescence, and then consider in more detail the contrasting experiences of two young people who spent long periods in different types of secure unit. Having previously placed the role of secure accommodation for young people in its wider contexts and also tried to identify a number of key ideas to help think about the meaning of what goes on in a secure unit, the following material provides a crucial link with the coming chapters which focus on practice and management issues.

Tell Them So They Listen

Tell Them So They Listen is a powerful piece of research conducted by the Trust for the Study of Adolescence and published as a research study by the Home Office. It recounts the findings of a series of focus groups with young offenders in a number of Young Offender Institutions, and includes contributions from young men and young women aged between 15 and 20 years old. The participants were asked to discuss three areas: life before and leading up to entering prison; their experiences of custody; and their hopes, fears and plans for the future. It was intended that: 'within these areas ... young people would explore their experience of, and views on: parenting; local authority care; education; employment; housing; drug and alcohol use; violence and bullying; and the criminal justice system' (Lyon *et al.* 2000). In many respects the conclusions to be drawn from the research paint a dismal picture of the young people's experience of the professionals with whom they have come into contact and of how they have been treated by the systems intended to provide for their care. It is important reading for all those involved with young people, and particular attention should be paid to the comments that the young people make about their experience of the adults who are charged with the responsibility of looking after them. The report identifies a number of key messages from the young people about their experiences and their hopes for the future. Four main themes emerge: choice and responsibility; parenting and families; professional adults and professional services; decent lives and decent futures.

> While many of their [the young people's] ideas for change require action by others, young people believe that principally it is up to them to change their own lives .... From discussion in the groups, a more complex picture developed. There had been times when many young people felt seriously let down by adults who could have cared for them or helped them .... Their emphasis on personal responsibility would endorse the development of institutional cultures which stress pro-social behaviour and citizenship.
>
> (ibid.: 78)

> In all the groups the young people talked a lot about their families. Many spoke of disrupted lives; absent fathers, premature deaths and changing family relationships .... Most were trying to maintain links with family and close friends while in prison .... Most young people did not want to see parents blamed for their children's involvement in crime.
>
> (ibid.: 79)

> Above all, young people wanted to be treated with respect in a way appropriate to their age and developmental stage. They wanted to be taken seriously by professional adults. Many gave detailed practical examples of disrespectful treatment, clear abuse of power by adults in authority and in some cases incidents involving overt racism or violence .... Almost all the young people said they wanted the professional adults who care for them to be people who they can respect .... They wanted people who were reliable and straightforward.

Constant personnel changes, particularly in probation and youth justice services were heavily criticised.

(ibid.: 80)

The young people defined what they regarded as decent lives and decent futures .... There would be good opportunities for education and health care. Young people would have real jobs and be paid properly. Above all, there would be no drugs, no homelessness, no poverty and no crime.

(ibid.: 80)

There are many important similarities between the views expressed by the young people about the reasons for their involvement in offending behaviour, their hopes for the future and the findings of research. Social factors such as the pressures on family life which come from poverty, poor housing conditions and lack of employment opportunities; a family history of involvement in crime; the influence of alcohol and drugs; low achievement in education and delinquent peer groups – these are all identified by the young people as contributing to their involvement in offending and reflect the themes that run through all the major research projects. It is also interesting to note the young people's views about the importance of their families and of maintaining contact with them whilst in custody, and the significance of positive adult role models to whom they can relate but who so often have been absent from their lives in any consistent or reliable way. Although the tone of many of the messages is negative, there is an underlying hope coming from the groups which is expressed in the aspirations that the young people have for their futures. They want a different and a better life for themselves. They can also see the ways in which this might be achieved and which do not entail continuing involvement in criminal behaviour. Important work can be done in secure units if the young people are actively engaged in the programme and offered positive opportunities for change. Their own views confirm how important the adults are in these settings in enabling that process to begin.

The stories of two young people

Joanne and Stephen are young people who throughout their adolescence spent considerable periods of time in secure units. Their stories illustrate many of the previous points made about children and young people who, because of what happens to them in their families, find themselves enmeshed in the complex networks of welfare and justice agencies and the professional adults who inhabit them. Their individual stories are unique and in thinking about them we are able to explore the connections between individuals and those systems which so often provide the stage upon which key relationships are made and subsequently evolve.

With Joanne and Stephen, understanding the developmental nature of those key relationships was essential for managing them safely and providing appropriate care and interventions. They both had very traumatic and disturbed early family experiences, including witnessing and suffering severe violence at the hands of carers, and multiple placements in care settings. With the onset of adolescence Joanne and Stephen displayed increasingly violent and sexualised behaviours towards their peers and adults. In the many secure units in which they were placed over periods of time they presented very difficult problems of management and provoked strong and often contradictory feelings in the adult carers. These feelings ranged from absolute helplessness and wanting to 'get rid' of them – often expressed as 'we can't do any more he/she needs specialist help and we don't have the expertise' – to an almost crusading sense of wanting to rescue and save them. This latter feeling was invariably accompanied by an unshakeable belief that 'only I can do this'. Joanne and Stephen also provoked enormous conflict between the different agencies involved in their care and management, and with Joanne this was further complicated by the destructive and hostile actions of her family.

In order to try and capture the sense of what involvement with these two young people was like for the staff in the secure units where they lived, it is important to remember that we are not describing a laboratory experiment. The day-to-day exchanges and encounters between staff and the young people, their families and the different professional groups involved, occurred at specific times and places. Each of these encounters both reflected a history and also contributed to the continuing story. The way in which these exchanges impacted on the people involved reflects the vast scope of human experiences and emotions. In the day-to-day there was a sharing of very ordinary things and some very special events; there was humour and sadness, hope and despair, with moods often changing rapidly and unexpectedly. Human strengths and frailties existed alongside each other as they do for most of us most of the time. A case study is useful for learning but it should never be forgotten that it is the lives of individual young people that are being described and that the ordinary human experiences of those young people have a significance that requires understanding and inclusion in any search for a sense of meaning or purpose in the events that took place during their time in secure units.

Joanne's story

Whilst still only aged 13 years Joanne was sentenced to custody for twenty-seven months for the offences of aiding and abetting rape and false imprisonment. She was the youngest child of Mary Lee and Bill Jones. Mary Lee had a child from a previous relationship, Alan Lee who was 21 years old. Joanne had a brother, Philip, who was 20 and a sister, Clare, who was 16 years old. The first agency to become involved with the family was social services, to whom Ms Lee turned when the two boys were aged 7 and 8 years. The reason for this self-referral was the difficult behaviour of the boys which was becoming out of the family's control. This behaviour included an episode of fire setting. Mary Lee and Bill Jones had a long history of domestic violence which began when the children were young, and Mary and the children repeatedly fled from their home and spent time in refuges. Joanne and her siblings had made a number of allegations of physical abuse against Bill Jones, and her older brothers were on the child protection register whilst they were in the care of Mr Jones and Ms Lee.

Joanne was accommodated by social services at the age of 13 years as she was deemed to be out of control, absconding frequently from the family home and reportedly involved in prostitution and drug abuse. Whilst accommodated by social services Joanne continued to abscond and there were serious concerns that she was still involved in prostitution and drugs. The offences for which she was later sentenced occurred during this period. Joanne lured a girl, slightly younger than herself, to a flat where she gave her alcohol and threatened her with violence if she tried to leave. The girl was subsequently raped by a man who was also in the flat.

Joanne was placed in local authority secure accommodation for nearly nine months prior to conviction. As she had received bail for her offences, her placement at this time was made on the grounds of 'welfare' reasons rather than a remand order. This meant that on receiving a custodial sentence no account could subsequently be made for this period in secure accommodation, as only time spent in a secure unit on a remand order is considered for the purposes of calculating the time to be spent in custody post-sentence. During this time pre-conviction Joanne was maintaining her plea of not guilty and, quite properly, as with all young people in this situation, no direct work could be undertaken with regard to the specific circumstances of the offence, and only a general preparation could be undertaken for her forthcoming court appearance. However, the grounds for Joanne's placement in secure accommodation related directly to her behaviour during the time at which the offence was alleged to have been committed and the danger that she was seen as presenting to herself and others. This ambiguity in the reasons for her placement created some powerful tensions between the secure unit staff and the social service professionals, with strong differences of opinion being expressed about her dangerousness and the meaning of her placement in secure accommodation. The views of the secure unit staff were fuelled by the day-to-day difficulties that they were having at this time in caring for her, and the way in which these difficulties manifested themselves through her challenging, manipulative and at times dangerous behaviour. Social services had a much less clear view about the nature of Joanne's difficulties and, from the point of view of the secure unit staff, seemed to be over-critical about the approach that was being taken with regard to her care. For their part, the field social workers believed the unit to be over-restrictive in its management approach to Joanne, and poor in communicating information and plans.

Joanne lived as part of a small group with four other girls, mixing with the boys' groups, who were accommodated in separate living units, only in education or organised social activities. In the early months of her placement Joanne was frequently loud and uninhibited. She would try to dominate group settings by prolonged outbursts of sexualised verbal abuse directed against staff of both gender. She was a very controlling young person around whom most of the unit activity and life needed to revolve, and she achieved this focus of attention through highly antisocial behaviour. Such were the levels of this that there were a number of discussions

within the staff team about the 'appropriateness' of the placement and a real ambivalence in the establishment as a whole
about whether or not she should return after sentence if
found guilty. Some of this was undoubtedly a result of her
constantly demanding behaviour, but there was considerable
ambivalence in the team about the nature of the offence, and
discussions about this evoked powerful feelings of revulsion
from some staff. On the other hand there were those who
engaged well with Joanne and with whom she appeared able to
relate more easily. They persisted in their views about the
viability of the placement and the possibility that it could help
her. There were observed differences in the way that she
approached male and female adults in the unit. Towards
women she was invariably hostile and on occasions aggressive
and violent. Towards men she alternated between flirtation
and anger. This was particularly observable in her relationship
with her male key worker who was both the object of her
anger but also someone to whom she could speak as she
slowly came to know him and gave him a measure of trust.

During the period before sentence there was very little
change in her overt behaviour, but after sentence there were
marked differences. Joanne became calmer and quite soon
began to use opportunities for talking about what had happened in the offence and how she felt about it, which was
actually pretty remorseful and ashamed. She slowly came into
more trusting relationships with staff and became closer to a
number of female staff with whom she was able to talk and
share activities. Aspects of her behaviour continued to be
worrying but without the extremes of aggression that had
characterised it before, and the day-to-day life of the residential unit provided opportunities for some very productive
work. At one time it was observed that Joanne was grooming
newly admitted girls for introductions to certain boys in the
unit to whom she had already made advances about their likely
interest in the newcomers. This provided a very immediate
way of linking to the circumstances of her offence and an
opportunity for this to be confronted in a safe way. It is an
example of how the immediate here and now can be used to

highlight issues of real therapeutic value and provide a locus for the kind of corrective emotional experience we have described previously. Joanne also used art therapy sessions to begin to explore more about her relationships with both males and females and also about her own sexuality and development as a young woman, which were all central to understanding the nature of her involvement in the offence and connected deeply to the role she had been forced to take on in her family.

Following Joanne's conviction case management responsibility was transferred from social services to the prison service. This also contributed to a change in the dynamics of the relationships between the professionals involved with Joanne. From her point of view, a more distant external authority was introduced from whom permission needed to be sought for aspects of her programme to be implemented. In the later stages this included 'mobility', which is the term used to describe the opportunity for a young person serving a long sentence in a local authority secure unit, under the supervision of staff, to leave the unit for short periods of time either for an educational visit or to prepare for resettlement into the community on release. This was for Joanne, as it is for most young people in these circumstances, an important development in her programme and one which she had to earn. Applying for permission to have mobility represented an opportunity for Joanne to test out whether or not an external authority would be fair and keep its word in exchange for her co-operation in taking more responsibility for her behaviour. From the unit's perspective, there was a greater clarity about the structure within which they were able to work, and also the finding of guilt meant that a legitimate focus could now be given to offence-focused work. As Joanne was now formally sentenced, her local youth justice team became involved in her programme in the secure unit, with the added responsibility for managing her after release on licence. The youth justice staff worked alongside social services and this also contributed to a more structured approach to the planning processes.

The clue to many of the difficulties that existed between

those involved in Joanne's care and management is perhaps most readily found by exploring closely the complex family relationships in which she was entangled and the way in which the agencies took on something of the key roles played out in her family drama. As she became more trusting of staff in the secure unit Joanne began to speak about her relationship with her father in which she had not only suffered physical abuse but had from an early age also been exploited sexually, and not only by him but by his friends as well. Visits from both her father and mother to the unit had been fraught from the beginning and were often accompanied by periods of very difficult behaviour from Joanne towards staff. Her parents' relationship remained stormy through the two years Joanne was in the secure unit, although by the end of the sentence Ms Lee had once again left Mr Jones and this time it seemed likely to be more permanent.

Joanne found in the secure unit the protection that her mother had not been able to provide, and at one point actually found the strength to refuse further contact with her father. This caused him great annoyance and anger which was displayed in hostility towards the unit staff and also in various complaints he made to the prison service about the treatment his daughter was receiving in the secure unit. Ms Lee was a regular visitor to her daughter and staff observed her to be 'more like the daughter than the mother' as she would dress similarly to Joanne and, seen together, they certainly appeared more like sisters than mother and daughter. Within the unit Joanne found male and female staff who behaved towards her in ways that were different from anything she had experienced before. This enabled her to begin to trust adults and to find ways of relating to them that were neither exploitative nor treated them as objects for her anger. Her own level of self-esteem also increased in the settled and protective environment that could actually keep her safe from the intrusions of her father and provide her with age-appropriate activities and education in which she thrived. Her relationship with her mother remained ambivalent but close and it was to her mother that she returned to live on release.

Joanne's placement in a local authority secure unit enabled a great deal of detailed and individual work to be undertaken. Her behaviour had contributed towards a serious sexual offence being committed but in the secure setting this could be understood from different points of view. It was not just an act of sexual aggression but an expression of anger by a young woman who herself had been physically and sexually abused and needed help in coming to terms with this and in making some decisions about how things were to be in the future.

Stephen's story

Stephen was 15 years old when he received a custodial sentence of four years for an indecent assault on a female care worker. His subsequent experience of being in a secure unit was to prove very different from Joanne's. Although he was placed initially in a local authority secure unit, his behaviour could not be safely contained in this setting and early on in the sentence he was transferred to a Young Offender Institution. During his period in custody Stephen was moved between establishments on six occasions and finally served just over three years of his total sentence. In the here and now of the secure setting Stephen was a continual management problem for staff and persistent in his attempts to disrupt the normal routines of the unit. Incidents involving Stephen included setting fire to his cell, intimidation of officer staff, particularly female officers to whom he would address sexualised comments whilst masturbating in front of them. Following a period of some intensive work with a probation officer in preparation for his attendance on a sex offender treatment programme he indecently exposed his erect penis and attempted to rub himself against her. He would also threaten and assault other young people whom he perceived as weaker and more vulnerable than himself. On other occasions his demanding and uninhibited behaviour would result in him being bullied and assaulted by his peers, making it very difficult for him to live in a group setting. The result of all this was that Stephen spent long periods of time in various 'segregation' units away from other young people and off what is described in prison as 'normal location'. It was at these times that he achieved his most stable behaviour and staff could comment on that other side of Stephen which was charming and personable. Ironically the routines of a segregation unit provided Stephen with a setting that made him feel safe, and this was an important clue as to the kind of environment in which he might have been more responsive and able to accept the help being offered. Stephen needed a high level of predictability in his daily life with some focused and specific attention provided for him by known and reliable adult staff. For a while, one establishment, through the endeavours of the psychology and education departments, managed to provide some structured activity for Stephen whilst he was in the segregation unit. This input came from the initiative of individual staff who took a particular interest in Stephen, but their efforts were not able to be incorporated into a wider programme. In the end the staff involved moved on or had other duties, and Stephen was also moved on as the 'placement' in the unit could not be sustained. Stephen had no visitors whilst he was in custody. His family had long since abandoned him, increasing his undoubted sense of isolation which was confirmed for him by the nature of the segregation units in which he spent a good deal of time.

Stephen's period in custody was characterised by frequent changes of placement which made it impossible to develop any overall strategy to engage him in a programme of treatment. Stephen brought a number of psychiatric assessments with him into custody and, whilst there, was assessed again. No formal diagnosis of mental illness could be made, although one report commented that he was 'too dangerous' for admission into a medium secure regional unit. Although there were staff in different Young Offender Institutions who thought that he could be engaged in individual work and did have some capacity to think about himself, they received neither the time nor the support for this to happen. The prison officers and their managers were much more doubtful about the possibilities of treatment and more concerned about how they could provide a safe environment for Stephen, other young people and themselves. They did not have the resources to organise a programme around his needs or the experience to think about how this might be done. They could only deal with the day-to-day problems he caused, and in the end moving him on and sharing the load was seen as the best solution. A much more positive aspect of Stephen's time in custody was the way in which the different agencies involved in his care and management were able to work together and plan for his release. It was acknowledged that little by way of treatment had been provided for him whilst in custody and consequently he would present as highly dangerous on release. This was confirmed by Stephen himself who was explicit about what he intended to do to members of his family and also about his fixation with a particular young woman he had previously known. A placement was identified for him after a great deal of effort by the probation service and this was supported with some additional central funding.

Prior to receiving his custodial sentence Stephen was living in a children's residential unit, his eighth placement since the age of 10. He was described as having begun to form relationships with a number of the staff group, and because of that the staff team were taken by surprise when the incident occurred. The other young people were out of the unit on a trip and Stephen, left alone with one member of staff, took the opportunity to commit a serious assault. He was 14 years old when this happened and, contrary to the beliefs of the staff team in that final residential placement, this was a culminating event of a severely disturbed childhood.

Reports describe Stephen's own father as having had no settled home of his own until aged 14 years and as having been the victim of violent parents. Stephen's mother also came from an unsettled and violent family background with a history of mental illness in a number of family members. Through a combination of their own difficulties and Stephen's early behavioural problems his parents were unable to care properly for him and from the age of 3 onwards he was placed in a series of different foster homes, residential special schools and children's homes. Before the custodial sentence Stephen had a total of sixteen placements including two short spells in secure accommodation. An early report indicated that at the age of 4 he showed an 'over-maturity' in his approach to adults and in his general behaviour, but an overview of the many reports provided about Stephen shows a remarkable catalogue of antisocial behaviours exhibited in all of the settings in which he was living. He is described as disruptive, aggressive towards other children and having boundless energy. A number of reports commented on his constant seeking out of adult attention and his ability to present himself as 'charming'. As Stephen got older the antisocial behaviour included sexualised acting out, often in a planned and systematic way which seemed intent on causing the maximum fear in his victims. This acting out was accompanied by an increasing frequency of delinquent behaviour and court appearances, with episodes of fire setting, theft and possession of offensive weapons, ending up at the age of 14 with the custodial sentence for indecent assault. Various psychiatric assessments made reference to Stephen's lack of remorse about events, his display of high levels of anger and frustration and his idealisation of his absent parents. The conclusions drawn in the reports were that he was suffering from a severe mixed disorder of conduct and attachment.

Although there can be no doubt that Stephen could be very difficult to look after, the complete absence of any consistent adult figure in his life is staggering. At different times and in different places there were significant adults for Stephen, but in almost every case the relationship ended abruptly and often as a result of something he did which triggered his removal from the situation. These adults clearly connected with Stephen and were for a short time able to draw out those positive aspects which are alluded to in the reports which now constitute his history. It is important to note how in so many respects what happened to Stephen in the secure units where he served his sentence replicated earlier childhood experiences. These include most tellingly the way he would act out before either he became too close to someone or they to him. This acting out usually involved highly sexualised, disruptive antisocial behaviours which would destabilise his living environment and frequently lead to a change of placement. Of course it should not be surprising that these patterns of behaviour continued. It is unfortunate, however, that none of the various custodial settings in which he was placed – a local authority secure unit and various Young Offender Institutions – was able to provide the necessary containment to challenge them. Neither were they able to engage Stephen in the necessary work required for him to think about his circumstances and move towards change. Individual staff did make the important connections between what was happening in the here and now and earlier experiences but the secure units were never able to develop a holistic approach to understanding the nature of Stephen's difficulties or to offer any co-ordinated strategy to begin to address them.

Joanne and Stephen are examples of young people who share the experience of a traumatic childhood and react to this by violent and deviant behaviours which finally result in prison sentences. Their behaviour presented considerable challenges to those staff charged with managing and looking after them whilst they were in secure units. They created enormous anxieties in the staff teams and in various ways perplexed and divided the different professional groups involved in the broader and longer-term processes of planning for their care. The ability of the secure units to look after them properly depended finally on the extent to which the staff groups could tolerate and contain the immediate problems arising from their behaviour. The next steps would have been to try to understand the nature of their difficulties from a developmental perspective in order to introduce a programme that could assist with bringing about some sort of change. For Joanne her placement in a local authority secure unit worked well, as the smaller environment was able to contain her appropriately and safely, and the setting could be used by the staff team to engage her, although not without a struggle, whilst slowly moving forwards in a process of change. For Stephen this was not to happen. None of the secure units in which he was placed could get much beyond the stage of containing him in a physical way that kept him and others safe in the secure setting. There was certainly no continuity of significant adult relationship and seemingly no capacity within the system for this to be thought about and implemented.

These examples highlight differences that exist in secure accommodation provision for young people and the importance of the Youth Justice Board's task to ensure that the necessary resources and services are made available for these most needy of young people in the right place at the right time. This is about more than just resources, however. It is about having an overall model of what work should be undertaken with problematic and dangerous young people whilst they are in secure units, and what kinds of support and training are needed by the residential staff who have the job of caring for them day to day. We have seen that for workers in secure units it is essential that they should have access to a body of ideas about human growth and behaviour and be encouraged to develop the capacity to use those ideas to think about what certain behaviours might mean in the here and now with particular individuals or groups. This needs to be linked to knowledge about the multiple factors that contribute to the development of delinquent and antisocial behaviour. In addition, staff need to understand the particular role that secure units play in relation to other agencies across the justice and welfare systems, and how different professional groups operate within these. It is this knowledge and understanding that provides the base which staff need to develop the wide range of skills that they require in order to engage effectively with young people in the units and to perform the complex tasks that they are expected to undertake.

Chapter 5

What happens inside?
Part I

> Children have never been very good at listening to their elders, but they have never failed to imitate them. They must, they have no other models.
>
> (James Baldwin)

The relationships that a young person manages to establish with other young people and with the members of staff who look after them on a daily basis are amongst the critical factors which determine what they achieve in the course of their placement in a secure unit. The significance of these relationships has been increasingly recognised in research findings (Liebling *et al.* 1999) and is reflected in a number of official reports, prison service orders and good practice guidelines. In a summary of what constitutes effective practice in secure units, Cosgrave emphasises the importance of staff in modelling positive behaviour for young people and draws attention to the levels of knowledge and skill that they require:

> The research shows that reinforcement and modelling of positive behaviours should be an important feature of work with young people. It further suggests that an effective pro-social modelling approach requires highly skilled staff, set in a context where work can be monitored. This work, while being the least visible, is in fact the most demanding, requiring constant vigilance, understanding and focus. Most of the day-to-day contact in secure facilities is by care staff or prison staff and, while many have excellent child care skills, this approach requires a more sophisticated level of knowledge and skill than generally they are expected to possess.
>
> (Cosgrave 2000)

In a comparative study of regimes in different types of secure unit, Ashmore found that staff in all settings saw 'consistency, respect and the importance of the relationship between staff and the young men as significant' (Ashmore 2000: 56). Cosgrave is undoubtedly right in recognising that these relationships, particularly those between young people and staff, cannot be left to chance or regarded as coincidental. Staff need to engage actively with young people both through their work with individuals and also when carrying out their routine duties which are part of group life. To be effective, modelling of pro-social behaviour should not be confined to sessions of social skills training but apparent through the way staff behave in the ordinary activities of the group day. In fact these routine activities have greater meaning for young people as they more closely replicate situations and interactions that happen outside the institution. The relationships that staff develop with young people in secure units are beneficial on a number of different levels. At their deepest they are intrinsically valuable for the experience that they offer to a young person through having contact with an adult who treats them fairly and with respect. In this regard they are enormously significant for the development of a young person's self-esteem and sense of well-being.

The relationship that a member of staff has with a young person is also an important factor in motivating and supporting other areas of their programme during the time spent in a secure unit. The purpose of modelling behaviour is for another person to see the effect that the behaviour has and by imitation to adopt it as their own when dealing with similar circumstances. To this extent the relationships that staff form with young people are instrumental in that they are intended to impact directly upon a young person's behaviour and to provide them with alternative responses in problematic situations. It is evident that this is most likely to be effective when there is a mutual respect in the relationship and when the adult modelling the behaviour is well regarded. It is also timely to remember that young people have a powerful effect on other young people and, therefore, can also be influential as positive or negative role models. This is why it is important in secure settings for staff to ensure that the overall environment promotes positive values and that status in the unit is gained through conformity to those values and not through flouting them. It is also why staff have to remain vigilant as guardians of the values and of their expression in the life of the unit, particularly when most young people are only staying for short periods of time. It follows from the complexity of the task that the skills involved in pro-social modelling require a specific training input and that for this to be fully effective the acquisition of skills must be closely linked to learning about child development and adolescent behaviour.

The core business

Secure units are living institutions in which groups of adults and young people come together in a tangle of relationships from out of which a considerable amount of emotional energy is generated. These relationships influence what happens to a young person during their time in a secure unit, and in order to engage in them effectively residential staff require a level of understanding and skills that may not be readily gained through participation in traditional training courses. They also require a range of personal qualities, including resilience and humour, which may not be easily measurable in the standard recruitment processes through which they have to pass when they apply for a job in a secure unit. Residential staff, whose daily work is to look after young people, mainly operate in the here and now and deal with issues and events that occur in the routines of daily group living. They have to be able, however, to understand current behaviour in the light of its origins and development over time so as to give meaning to its immediate expression and manage its consequences. The ways in which a young person's earlier experiences and the associated traumas are constantly re-enacted provide the raw material which staff have to absorb and manage on a daily basis. The challenge for staff of being able to contain this raw material in a way that keeps the secure unit safe and at the same time allows them to provide some feedback to the young people is at the core of their work. It is also central to the processes whereby the potential and often actual chaos of a unit is gradually transformed into a culture that offers containment, safety and opportunities for personal growth and development.

The Youth Justice Board is clear that the work of secure units is to address directly the offending behaviour of young people and to deliver programmes that reduce the likelihood of its reoccurrence on release. The involvement of all staff in this process is essential if the objective is to be achieved. This primary aim is linked to a set of standards about what a daily regime in a secure unit should consist of, along with stated expectations about the number of hours that young people must spend in various activities during the course of a day. The core staff groups in local authority secure units and secure training centres are the residential care workers, or their equivalent namesakes, and in the prison service they are the prison officers. These are the key staff for the delivery of the daily regime and they are supported by a range of other professionals who are involved in different aspects of a young person's programme, such as education or specialist offending behaviour programmes. The required high level of direct involvement by staff with the young people during the course of a day's activities has long been a regular feature of the work of residential workers in local authority secure units and an expectation of staff in secure training centres since their opening. It has not been a feature of the work of prison officers, whose traditional role has been much more about the performance of tasks in order to ensure that routines take place, that prisoners are delivered to wherever they are expected to be and that security is maintained. Prisoners spend long periods of time either in their cells or occupying themselves while watched over by prison officers. It has only been since April 2000 that a specific set of prison orders has existed to provide directives to staff about the particular needs of the younger adolescent population in their charge, and that this group has been accommodated separately from older prisoners. The standards required by the Youth Justice Board have presented the prison service with a whole new set of challenges which they have had to confront, about how care, management, education and offending behaviour programmes are best provided to their youngest population, i.e. those aged 15 to 18 years. The exposure of prison officers to the kind of pressures that come from having to engage closely with a disturbed and delinquent adolescent population in a secure setting is relatively new for the prison service organisation. It is therefore critically important that not only does the prison service develop the right kind of residential accommodation and other facilities for young people in custody, but that they also attend to the training and support needs of their staff groups.

Differences between staff groups

Although general reference has been made throughout to staff and to staff groups it is important to acknowledge that there are many different groups of staff working in secure units. These groups come from a wide range of backgrounds, hold a number of different professional qualifications, have varying levels of experience and perform distinctive functions. In addition to the multi-disciplinary professional staff groups who provide direct care, management, education and treatment programmes, there are also administrative, catering, facilities management and domestic staff. These latter groups, although not necessarily involved directly with young people, have essential roles to play in the delivery of a secure unit's overall regime. As these staff carry out their duties they also come into contact with young people and may form significant relationships with them. In any event, simply by working in a secure unit these staff become part of its network of relationships and subject to its prevailing pressures.

An organisational factor which has to be taken into account and which can affect relationships between staff groups is the disparity that exists between them in the terms and conditions of employment. This may arise from the different status of the groups in terms of those who are directly employed by the establishment as against those whose services are contracted. It may also arise from perceived differences in professional status which are reflected in salary levels or annual leave entitlements. The most obvious example, which has been a thorn in the side of many managers in local authority secure units over the years, is in the comparability of the employment conditions for teachers and those for residential care staff. In the prison service there are similar tensions between prison officers and contracted education services. However, there are real tensions within the ranks of prison service personnel around the issue of status, and in particular the degree of recognition afforded to prison officers whose performance of many of the routine tasks does not seem to them to be duly acknowledged. These are structural factors and although there have been attempts to address these differentials there has not been any single successful resolution to the underlying problem. Managers of secure units in all sectors are unlikely to be able to eliminate these differences in their establishment, but they can have an important influence on the extent to which they impact on its functioning. Arguments about terms and conditions often seem to surface at times when there is real stress amongst staff or in the institution as a whole, and usually become a focus when a particular group of staff feels marginalised.

Billy was a young person who had spent a number of different periods in secure accommodation. His behaviour was unpredictable but what was most frustrating for staff was the fact that he seemed incapable of learning from experience or of retaining information for more than a few minutes at a time. His behaviour annoyed and irritated other young people on the unit and, although he could have violent outbursts which were directed at both staff and young people, he was more usually constantly demanding, asking questions, unable to settle to any activity without individual staff support, picking things up, breaking items around the unit, particularly anything electrical, and a continual presence in a way that drove staff to distraction. A few staff were more able than the rest to be alongside Billy during his waking hours, and they became a small team allocated to trying to make some sort of programme come together for him. This team included a couple of the domestic staff for whom Billy seemed to have a certain affection and, when on the living unit, they spent a limited amount of time with him. Clearly Billy's behavioural difficulties did not make him an ideal candidate for formal educational activities and so it was not too long after his admission that he was excluded from the educational facility in the secure unit. Teachers declared him to be unteachable and required that Billy should be looked after by residential staff; although work would be provided, he could not be accommodated in lessons. Given how demanding it was to look after Billy and the drain this put not just on individual staff but on the resources of the team as a whole, it soon became a fiercely debated point as to who earned what and for what purposes salaries were paid.

In trying to counteract this kind of dispute it is essential to establish a strong set of values in which respect for all staff, irrespective of their role, is accepted as a norm and lived out in management practice. Identifying these potential sources of tension and talking about them provide important information about what is currently going on in an institution and the nature of the underlying feelings that are being expressed. In the case of Billy a great deal of talking was required between the different staff groups to understand their respective positions and to try to locate some understanding of what was going on in the particular needs and situation presented by Billy.

Vehemently expressed concerns about terms and conditions may also be thought about as an example of what could be described as low institutional self-esteem and how this is acted out by staff groups from time to time. Understanding these feelings in this way links directly back to our earlier discussion about wider perceptions of secure units and the impact that these may have on staff.

The overarching arrangements for the management of secure units, whether they be in the local authority, prison service or independent sector, vary considerably and consequently impact on staff in different ways. Despite these differences the fact is that all staff who are employed in a secure unit face similar issues, and the common features that arise from working alongside others in different roles and in settings where the primary task is looking after highly delinquent and disturbed young people raise concerns and problems that override overall organisational structures. On those all too rare occasions when staff from different parts of the secure estate come together it is interesting to note how quickly they establish a common agenda about what it is like to work in secure units. This is usually expressed in terms of how demanding the young people are, how their volatile behaviour is very hard to manage and the effect that this has on them as staff.

Working in teams

In spite of the attention given to the needs of individual staff and the high levels of support that they require, it should be remembered that the main locus of work in secure units is in teams. This is as true for staff who provide support services as it is for those whose core daily work involves direct contact with young people. Individual staff may belong to more than one team in their secure unit. As well as being part of the whole staff group they may also belong to a house or wing team and work with a small group of colleagues in a shift team. There is an obvious organisational imperative for the use of teams of staff in residential care settings, namely the necessity to provide staffing cover for twenty-four hours each day of the year. The use of shifts to provide cover is an important feature of the working pattern for staff in secure units. Their expressed attitudes and feelings about the 'roster' or the 'detail', as it is called in the prison service, can generally be taken as a barometer of staff morale. Many staff meetings have been used to vent feelings about the duty roster which, if given careful consideration, invariably reveal a good deal about what is happening in the unit and the reasons why staff are feeling angry or despondent. Staff use the roster as a measure of the extent to which their managers are demonstrating their understanding and concerns about the difficulties they face in their work. Negotiating changes to the roster or the detail is a big deal and occupies many hours of management and staff time.

In the early history of residential care this was not an issue as staff were expected to live in the residential home and there were no clear-cut distinctions between work and off-duty times. There are still some examples of this approach in smaller, independent children's homes but not in the public sector. The 'industrialisation' of the working conditions for staff in residential care has ended any expectations that staff should be on duty at all times and there are good reasons for this. It is essential that staff have interests and relationships outside of the residential setting, but there is an ongoing consequence in that the comings and goings of staff from shift to shift have an impact on the young people. Their interest in the organisation of the roster is no less intense than that of the staff.

'Who's on tonight?' is a question that is asked hundreds of times a day in secure units across the country. Its meaning reflects more than simply a passing interest for the young person who is asking. For them it represents an anxiety about their security and is a way of seeking re-assurance that they are not about to be abandoned. Although staff cannot be expected to work endless hours with no rhythm or pattern to their working week, they must remember that in terms of how the young people think about their presence on the unit the expectation is that the focus of all adult interest is on them and on life in the secure unit.

This can also be another source of stress for staff in secure units. The appetite of young people for information about the life of staff outside the secure setting is voracious. Their fantasising and imaginings sometimes appear intrusive to staff who are immediately faced with dilemmas about how much they can properly share about their life, and in particular their relationships, outside the work setting. Staff are caught between the extremes of saying nothing, which appears dismissive and unreal, or of revealing too much detail. If too much is revealed there is a serious pos-sibility that important boundaries will be eroded, and then the staff mem-ber finds that the young person has 'got inside them' in a way that is neither healthy nor helpful to either. It is an advanced skill to be able to use a young person's enquiries as part of a therapeutic exploration about the meaning of the question in terms of that young person's own experi-ence and in the context of their transference relationship with the staff member. Given the limitations of the training received by most staff, such an analysis might reasonably be considered to be beyond the scope of what should be expected from a member of staff in their individual relationship with a young person, whether that be as a key worker, per-sonal officer or in a similar professional role. However, as relationships deepen, a young person will as a matter of course become interested in personal aspects of the staff's lives. The development of techniques and ways of responding to these questions is important for all staff to consider and should be discussed by the whole team so that some agreed formula or way of dealing with this issue can be reached without either appearing artificial or encouraging over-familiarity. Different staff feel comfortable with different levels of self-disclosure, and the type of setting is also a factor in the way staff respond to this sort of enquiry by the young people. In all circumstances, however, there must be a common frame-work of understanding about the importance of these boundaries, which should not be crossed by any one member of the team. Team work is im-portant here as it is the vehicle whereby the young people can experience differences in adult responses but learn that there are boundaries to be observed, which clearly define acceptable and unacceptable behaviour. This applies across a number of areas and demonstrates the value of team work which supports individual members of staff in particularly difficult situations. The targeting of particular staff by young people is a corrosive feature of life in a residential unit. This is probably more true in smaller settings where there is a greater intensity in the staff presence, but it is always an intrusive and potentially demoralising experience for the staff concerned. The way in which a staff team responds to this can be most supportive for the staff member but it requires a mature approach by the team as a whole. As staff share the load with colleagues so young people are enabled to see a mix of qualities and skills existing in the staff group and consequently are able to have a much richer experience in their relationships with the adults in the secure unit.

In order for teams to function effectively they have to be organised and managed in ways that support the achievement of their aims and objectives. Issues to do with how complex organisations such as secure units are most effectively managed and how adequate systems can be designed to capture the full range and flavour of the material that they generate will be discussed later on in Chapter 6. From the point of view of the staff, however, there are three key features required: a clear vision about the purpose and value base of the unit; good communication systems; and a shared understanding of the tasks and roles they are required to perform. Establishing and maintaining the vision for an organisation and setting out a clear value base upon which all staff's actions and decisions are taken is a whole organisation task. Individual staff have to feel part of that process and that to some extent they have contributed towards it. This is not just a one-off activity for new organisations but requires regular attention. In any event all staff must be able to sign up to the values of the organisation in which they are employed and be prepared to make those values explicit in the way that they approach their work. Staff must also have confidence in the systems and mechanisms in place for ensuring good communication. This is vital for the exchange of information which may be critical for the safety of other staff and young people or for enabling proper decisions to be taken and actions to be followed through. Staff, however, also have to feel that within the organisation there are channels of communication that are sufficiently robust for their concerns to be passed on, and through which they can receive the necessary support in times of difficulty. How feelings are communicated in organisations is nowhere more important than in a secure unit where the feelings of staff are actually an important source of information about young people or indeed colleagues.

Devising systems which allow the articulation of expressions of feeling and uses them as part of management information is a sophisticated business. There are a number of important structures which need to be in place to ensure that there is a flow of information through the secure unit. In one secure unit a careful system of daily meetings was established for managers at the beginning and end of each day to provide a kind of 'book-end' for the day's business, and these short meetings became an important part of the way in which the management team provided containment for the staff groups. More formal and regular meetings between key managers are also essential and should overarch a system of meetings which staff from the various disciplines are able to attend in order to share and address common issues. Exactly how these meetings are arranged depends on a number of factors to do with the particular needs of the organisation.

These meetings also need to be linked to regular team meetings for those staff whose daily work is the direct care, management and education of the young people. Such meetings are essential and play an important part in the lives not only of the staff members but also of the young people for whom they represent another occasion on which their needs are being acknowledged. We have already discussed the ambivalence that these meetings can occasion in the young people's group, but for staff they are a key part of the routine of the week in terms of the opportunities that they afford for thinking and talking about the issues of the day. In that sense meetings play an important role not just in the containment of young people's anxieties but those of staff as well.

While responsibility for ensuring that these meetings occur rests with managers, there is also an onus on staff to ensure that they are prepared to participate as fully as possible. Often in residential situations, as elsewhere in organisational life, people may hold back in the formal opportunities that they have to air their views but then take the issues and voice their opinions outside of the meeting structure. This has enormous potential for damage and can be highly destructive to the team-building process to which the meetings are intended to contribute. The same principles apply to the daily handover meetings which are, or should be, a feature of work in secure units and which are essential in people organisations dependent on patterns of shift working. Whilst it is a management responsibility to ensure that the routine of the day includes the opportunity for those staff leaving shift to pass on key information to those arriving, it is staff's responsibility to be positive in their approach to handover meetings. The better models of practice for these meetings encourage an active interrogation of staff leaving the unit by those coming on, rather than relying on the departing staff to remember to list all the significant events of the preceding shift. Without a clear structure that enables staff to meet together, share information and reflect on their reactions as individuals and as a team, the inevitable problems which beset all organisations in this area of work will seem even more insurmountable. There are a number of common issues which all teams have to confront and which include: inter-personal differences and how these affect functioning; problems of team members who are persistently late or don't seem to be making a full contribution; frequent and high levels of short-term absence or sickness; facing up to difficult issues and dealing with them openly; managing inter-team rivalry and avoiding a culture where one's own success is measured in relation to another team's failures. Regular and well-led team meetings, which take place in a wider organisational context that acknowledges these sorts of issues, are essential if such matters are to be properly dealt with. There is a particular problem that occurs in secure units working with highly delinquent or disturbed young people and that is the issue of splitting. Examples have already been discussed about how this phenomenon occurs but it is important to remind ourselves of the powerful ways in which projection and transference influence how individuals or groups react and respond to events going on around them. Teams find themselves divided about how a young person or group of young people should be treated or about the meaning of their behaviour. Sometimes this clearly goes beyond professional differences of opinion and staff become more involved than they are aware in the internal worlds of the young people.

Joanne, the young person described in the case study in the previous chapter, is a good example of the way in which an individual can provoke strong feelings and reactions from a staff group. She was placed in a secure unit with a strong model of therapeutic work, and so in the regular weekly team meetings, which were facilitated by a clinical psychologist, her behaviour and its underlying messages were discussed. The strong feelings around Joanne were not reduced by this process, but at least they were openly confronted. On a number of occasions, usually following some particularly difficult incident, there were real calls for her placement to be ended as staff felt they had come to the end of the road. The splits in the staff team changed as the different presenting sides of Joanne's personality were considered. The critical issue, which in reality was never completely put on the table, focused around Joanne's sexuality and the effect that her provocative and sexualised behaviour was having on the male and female staff. It was easier to discuss this in the context of her relationships with the boys and girls on the living units, which came to the fore when it was realised that she was grooming newly admitted girls for the purposes of handing them over to the boys. On the other hand, making connections with how staff were feeling about the approaches that at another level were being made to them was much more difficult. The team could not look at what this might mean in terms of her experience of being parented and, in particular, the relationship with her mother. The staff group found it easier to talk about the more obviously violent behaviour she presented on occasions, and in these circumstances, depending on the object of her attacks, i.e. male or female staff, could recognise some of the acting out of the family dynamic.

Unless this kind of material is brought out into the open in a team setting where it can be thought about and staff can be helped to understand its significance, then at best important information is lost and at worst ill-informed casework decisions are made to the detriment of a young person. With Joanne the team meetings helped to air issues and to decide ways of trying to manage her more disruptive behaviour, as well as offering some opportunity for insight into what certain aspects of it might mean.

Staff supervision

Perhaps the most important vehicle through which staff receive support and guidance and also talk about the concerns that arise in the course of their work is that of supervision. Professional supervision in residential work is still very undeveloped in terms of suitable models and in the priority that is afforded to its delivery. Of course there are exceptions to this and there are units in which the practice of professional supervision for staff is well established. However, in the prison service, which as we have already seen looks after the majority of young people in secure accommodation in England and Wales, there is no model at all of professional supervision for prison officers who carry out the most essential tasks with the young people in the residential setting. The traditional model of supervision provides for staff to have the regular opportunity to take some time and space in which they can discuss issues to do with their professional work and in which they can receive feedback and support. This is not the same as managerial monitoring or performance appraisal, although the different processes may link with each other. Professional supervision of this sort depends on the availability of staff with sufficient experience and skills to act as supervisors, and this has traditionally been the problem for residential settings. The lack of structured and comprehensive training for staff entering residential work in any sector or setting, together with the absence of planned career progression, is a major contributory factor to the dearth of people with a sufficiently high level of professional expertise to perform the supervisory function.

Although there can be no doubting the benefit of staff having individual time, there are some serious questions to be raised about the appropriateness of this model, however, as the sole vehicle for staff supervision in residential settings. Many tasks in residential work are carried out by staff working as part of a group in what are public and shared spaces. Supervision models which provide opportunities for peer groups of staff to meet and talk can be most effective, if properly facilitated, and more closely reflect the working environment. The problem in developing this style of supervision is again likely to be one of not having sufficient numbers of qualified supervisors, as this use of group work methods does require yet another set of skills to be learned. Another useful model which can be more easily implemented is what has been described as on-line supervision, i.e. where a less experienced member of staff shadows a more experienced colleague and receives immediate feedback on their performance and responses. Although there are real problems about providing adequate numbers of qualified supervisors, serious consequences can be expected if there is no supervision system in place at all that offers staff an appropriately managed context in which they can both give and receive feedback about their work and, most importantly, talk about the effect that the work is having on them.

The ideal model for supervision in residential settings, including secure accommodation, is a combination of individual and group sessions, preferably involving the same supervisors and supervisees in each. Although issues of confidentiality from individual supervision should be respected, receiving support from an individual session often allows staff to raise issues with other team members that otherwise they might not have been able to do. This can be a powerful tool in helping a team of staff to manage particularly difficult young people, where what sometimes happens is that certain staff take the stance of 'I never have any problems with them'. This kind of response can be challenged most effectively by team members if they can be encouraged to say either what their own difficulties are or in what ways other staff are not helping the team effort by taking individual positions.

If there is little or no supervision and this is heightened by the absence or irregular occurrence of team or handover meetings, then it is highly likely that staff teams will develop their own maladaptive ways of managing the pressures engendered by this type of work, and these will provide a rife breeding ground for poor and even dangerous practice.

This could easily have happened with Joanne, who was a very powerful young person and quite capable of manipulating individual staff into either a collusive or indeed a more sexualised relationship. The constant supervision of individual staff working with her and the regular team meetings helped to avoid either situation developing.

Anxiety in organisations

Organisations whose main functions involve tasks which provoke high levels of anxiety in staff tend to develop work cultures and practices which defend against the full realisation of those anxieties breaking into the routines of the workplace. Isabel Menzies Lyth's research includes her well-known study of a hospital setting in which the working practices of nurses were organised in such a way as to shield them against the extreme feelings aroused by their work in dealing with life and death situations (Menzies Lyth 1959). Some of the defensive techniques she identified within the organisation included: splitting up the nurse–patient relationship; depersonalisation; categorisation and denial of the significance of the individual; detachment and denial of feelings; the attempt to eliminate decisions by ritual task performance. Examples of how these techniques are employed could be shown in secure institutions of almost every type. In prisons they would include: use of numbers instead of names or calling prisoners by their surnames; use of categorisation to describe types of prisoners, e.g. 'he's a Cat. A'; lack of choice in ordinary daily routines; over-reliance on procedures; inflexible application of rules and the denial of feelings in a macho culture that spurns supervision or staff support as a waste of time. The dangers inherent in these long-standing conventions have been recognised in the prison service orders that now regulate the working practices of staff with the younger age group in custody. However, there is still a sea change needed before they can finally be put to rest and this can only happen if an alternative organisational model is presented to staff in which they are able to have confidence. It is dangerous to take away the traditional methods or symbols used by prison officers to maintain their professional role, and which in their view are essential in maintaining good order and discipline, without putting credible and robust alternatives in their place.

Two examples of this are the removal of the standard prison service uniform and the change in rules about the adding of days on to sentence length as punishment for ill-discipline. In the early months of change these have been hotly debated issues in the prison service amongst staff working with the younger group. The removal of the authority to add days to sentences is a result of the rules accompanying the introduction of the Detention and Training Order. This has been experienced as a challenge to the authority of custodial staff in responding to bad behaviour. Other parts of the secure estate have never had the option to add days to sentences and have had to develop other strategies for managing challenging behaviour. Although the issue of uniform may not seem to be huge in itself, as we have already noted, in the world of secure units small things become big and may often be most clearly understood if taken to represent other important matters which are not so easily talked about. In both these cases the issue is about the nature of staff's relationships with young people and how they may exercise proper adult authority in their dealings with them. Staff in Young Offender Institutions working with 15- to 17-year-olds are now expected to have contact with young people throughout the full course of a day, and this comes with an expectation that this direct work is significant and important for the overall time the young person spends in the unit. The critical anxiety for staff is that by being drawn into inescapable contact with the young people, they are exposed to the raw emotionally charged material which they carry around with them and project out and into their adult carers. Arising from this anxiety comes the question that each member of staff has to answer: 'How do I cope with all this especially if those traditional barriers and buffers between myself and the young people are no longer in place?'

The prison service has the responsibility at the present time for looking after about 85 per cent of the young people under the age of 18 years who are placed in secure accommodation in England and Wales. It is therefore appropriate to focus on the specific needs of staff working with that group of young people in Young Offender Institutions. However, it should not be imagined that similar issues do not arise for staff working in the other secure settings in which young people are placed. Local authority secure units and secure training centres are much smaller than the average Young Offender Institution. Staff in these institutions also experience considerable levels of anxiety and express their concerns in much the same way as their prison service counterparts. The same question is asked: 'How do I cope with the effect that these young people are having on me?' The smaller size of the units enables a more individualised and personal approach to be taken in the delivery of primary care, first names are in common usage between staff and young people and there is a greater emphasis on the general welfare of each young person in the unit. Whereas in the prison service staff have traditionally defended against too much closeness to the young people by the way in which their prison officer role has been defined, in local authority secure units the work of staff is often specified in terms of their role as carers and through their relationships with the young people. However, these too can assume a defensive quality – for example, when staff are observed to collude with a young person in avoiding confrontation about the underlying deviant or antisocial nature of their behaviour. In these instances staff's attention becomes exclusively focused on satisfying at a superficial level a young person's immediate care needs.

Another extreme that occurs more frequently in this kind of secure setting is the over-involvement of individual staff with a young person, which may take various forms but generally involves a breaking down of boundaries around personal–professional divides. In these instances a member of staff may become too closely identified with a young person and their circumstances. For example, a casework decision has been taken for a young person to transfer from a particular secure unit, a process which carries with it an inevitable feeling of some sense of loss. Rather than helping the young person come to terms with this experience the member of staff carries that sense of loss and acts it out, perhaps by becoming inappropriately tearful or angry in meetings. This is a rather mild example of over-identification. More serious, and thankfully very rare, are those examples where the apparent mutual attraction between staff member and young person gets acted out through a physical or sexual relationship. In other cases a collusive relationship may develop between a young person and member of staff in which they pair up against the rest of the staff team to undermine and destroy what ought to be a whole staff team approach to that young person's management and to the issues that need to be addressed.

In all secure units, irrespective of their different organisational frameworks, the same core anxiety for staff exists around the potentially destructive effect that exposure to the young people might have. Allied to this anxiety is the commonly expressed view that there are never enough staff on duty at any one time. This is the case whether there are three staff on duty with sixty young people or four staff on duty with eight! In an informal survey carried out with staff groups in a secure unit, the two factors that were unanimously identified as the main sources of staff stress were a fear of being left alone in the secure unit and a fear of being attacked. The consequence of these anxieties is associated with a breakdown of order, loss of control and a descent into chaos. If staff believe they are likely to be overwhelmed, then it is very important for them to feel that they are in control of the environment and of any situation that may arise. These are familiar themes which almost always emerge in discussions with staff groups who work in secure settings, and in a way they are a different articulation of the concerns about numbers – i.e. if the greatest fears are of being alone and of being attacked by a volatile and dangerous group of young people and the consequence of this is a loss of control then there can in a sense never be 'enough' staff. Incidentally, this is the anxiety which I found so difficult to understand in the scenario at the beginning of this book and which Tom was able to exploit so effectively. My feeling of isolation was connected to the fantasy that senior managers and other staff had abandoned my colleague and me and we were literally alone in the face of unknown danger.

Organisations and individuals whose work creates high levels of anxiety are liable to develop strategies and working practices intended to reduce the effects of that anxiety. We have identified some of these practices and how they may operate in all secure units. We have also identified how underlying anxieties for staff are directly related to the particular groups of young people whom they look after and the kinds of problems and difficulties they present. Fear of being alone and of being attacked are the two main expressions of this anxiety and these are inextricably linked to what from time to time becomes an overpowering sense that if this were ever to happen the consequence would be a total breakdown of order and loss of control. Although there is a physical dimension to these fears and it is this that staff initially acknowledge, they also carry powerful psychological meanings which touch the deeply personal anxiety of what it is to be left alone or to be destroyed.

At this point we should note how these same feelings are mirrored in the experiences of young people and are just as relevant and important to them as they are to the adult group in secure units. Almost without exception these children and young people are very vulnerable and many of them share extreme difficulties in forming and maintaining relationships with others of their own age and with adults. We have seen previously how we are learning more about the ways in which these difficulties can frequently be traced back to very early poor or disrupted attachment experiences with key carer figures. Such emotional deprivation may well have been a recurring feature throughout their young lives, along with repeated episodes of being ill-treated by adult carers through physical or sexual abuse and sometimes both. We have also seen how such experiences affect young people's behaviour and the ways in which they respond to and treat adults. The experience of being admitted to a secure unit, unless it is sensitively managed, may only serve to increase anxieties about being alone and being attacked. Being in a secure unit can feel very much like being 'locked away' from familiar places or people and isolated from what is known. This may be accompanied by a real sense of loss by a young person, arising not just from their lack of contact with family and friends, but also from their loss of control over what is happening to them. In the routine of a secure unit this takes the form of lack of choice in the small everyday decisions about such things as when and what to eat or what to watch on television. These are only symbols, however, of the absence of real choice for a young person about important life matters regarding which, as a result of earlier experiences, their options have already been seriously limited. Spending long periods of time on their own in a small room or cell only exacerbates the fear of being alone and accentuates feelings of loss of control. It certainly does not provide opportunities to build relationships or engage in activities which promote personal development and growth. Similarly, the fear of attack or of being bullied, which is a common vehicle for violence in secure units, can be very real for young people. In the same way as staff without proper leadership and support develop potentially unhealthy and damaging ways to guard against their anxieties, so too do young people. In secure units the extreme forms of this involve a young person either becoming aggressive towards others or damaging themselves through self-harming behaviours. Sometimes for young people coming into secure units the apparent loss of control is experienced as a relief from the chaos of their recent lifestyles. Despite what might appear to be the case, young people do not really want chaos or disorder to disrupt the secure unit any more than the adult group. It is just as frightening for them to feel that they, or the situation around them, are out of control. Working towards giving appropriate controls back to young people and linking this to increasing their sense of personal worth and becoming more responsible in their attitudes and behaviour towards others is a vital part of the task for secure units. Initially, however, staff may have to take a good deal of responsibility for each young person in order to keep them and others around them safe. Or, to put it another way, staff need to think on behalf of the young person until they are in a calmer and more organised space to do it for themselves.

Managing conflict in secure units

Rather than allowing maladaptive ways of managing stress in secure units to become institutionalised in pointless routines and oppressive structures, there has to be a shared acknowledgement of its origins and nature. Fear of being alone and of being attacked, with a consequent breakdown of order, is shared by both adults and young people. A full understanding of what this actually means is essential for the proper management and care of the young people and as a basis for providing sufficient and appropriate support systems for staff. These issues are brought into sharp relief when the question is considered as to how conflict and differences get dealt with in secure units:

> The strategies and principles used by a society and all its organisations for dealing with disagreements and conflict reflect the basic values and philosophy of that society.
>
> (Likert 1976: 14)

In secure units conflict takes many forms and occurs between different groups: it may be between young people or between staff and young people; it may be between individual staff members, teams and groups of staff or between staff and management. Highly charged and powerful feelings and emotions are inevitably stirred up by very needy young people competing with each other for the one thing they crave in common, the attention of adults.

At whatever level in the organisation conflict occurs, the way in which it is resolved and dealt with is, as Likert observes, a telling indicator as to the basic values and principles upon which an organisation is founded. In secure units there are two areas in particular which are of great concern to staff and which are extremely contentious for contemporary practice. These are: those conflict situations where physical restraint is used by staff, and those which arise when allegations are made by young people about staff. In each setting within the secure estate, procedures are in place to govern the use of methods for the physical control of young people. In the prison service the use of physical restraint is highly regulated and staff are routinely trained in techniques that have been developed over a number of years. A similar situation exists for secure training centres where an approach has been developed based on techniques used in the prison service but specially adapted to be employed with young people. All staff are trained in the techniques, which are, however, firmly placed in a context of positive child care and the importance of relationships as the basis for interventions. The situation is a lot less clear in the local authority secure units, where there are no approved methods for the physical restraint of young people, and although there is a requirement to record incidents there are no standard national procedures as to how this should be done or how such incidents should be reviewed. The policies and procedures which prescribe good practice allow physical restraint to be used only as a last resort by staff in managing a young person's behaviour.

In residential settings the possible 'flash points' or 'triggers' for behavioural disturbance are in most cases capable of being anticipated. A staff group who know the young people in their care and provide for their needs in a reliable and consistent way are likely to be aware of factors that might be upsetting for each individual young person. This includes awareness of group tensions, including the potential for bullying, and ensuring that potentially distressing events such as family visits or case meetings are well prepared for and supported both during and after their occurrence. The policy for restraint to be used only as a last resort indicates that this is a behaviour management technique that should only be used when order has broken down and other means of resolving a conflict have been exhausted. This may seem to beg the question as to who decides at what point this stage has been reached and in what circumstances this decision can be made. There are clearly some situations where there is an immediate danger to young people or to staff and a physical intervention is required to avert serious harm. As there is no easy way to prescribe for all eventualities, in order to gain a more complete understanding of these issues it is necessary to take several steps backward and locate the use of physical control in the context of the prevailing culture within a secure unit. It is this culture which determines the routine ways in which problems are solved and the manner in which adults and young people behave towards each other. Such matters are a commonplace part of life and their handling reflects the way in which formal procedures and practices interact with a whole number of informal dynamics which are established between adults and young people in the day-to-day life of a secure unit. These formal and informal processes govern expectations about how people should behave towards each other when there are differences and conflicts to be sorted out. Robust and effective management is essential for: establishing a culture of respect with clear expectations about resolving problems and differences; setting out the boundaries around the use of physical control and making these clear to staff and young people; monitoring the use of physical control in the unit and supporting staff and young people when an incident occurs.

The use of physical methods to control young people involves techniques which have to be employed just at the moment when the profound underlying anxieties shared by both staff and young people about loss of control and fear of attack are in effect about to be realised. This is why such incidents spark so much intense anxiety and feeling. It is also why formalising training is so important, and staff need to be very well rehearsed in the application of whatever approved or agreed techniques are in operation in their unit. Maintaining a rigorous practice, in which only approved techniques may be used, assists staff in remaining detached and sensitive in situations where emotions are running high. A common mistake made by inexperienced staff, and to which more experienced colleagues are not immune, is that of personalising conflict with a young person. Disturbed young people have the uncanny knack of being able to direct the most telling personal insult guaranteed to provoke any adult with whom they come into contact and at the same time press just the right button to arouse the most extreme emotion, whether that be anger, frustration or just downright embarrassment. For staff to have the combination of personal maturity, professional knowledge and skill to withstand such an attack, which again can be guaranteed to come when they are feeling most vulnerable, is something not easily acquired but absolutely essential.

Any use of physical force by adults which necessarily involves taking hold of a young person is an assertion of power in its most basic and primitive form. Feelings and impulses of which a member of staff might be quite unaware easily surface and leave them and the young person aroused and anxious. It is therefore essential to ensure that after any incident there is a thorough debrief for all concerned and that everyone involved is able to have an opportunity for reflection about how things have been left and what needs to be done in the aftermath to rebuild relationships. This process of debriefing is different from the important task of ensuring that a proper written record is made of every incident involving the use of force, which can then be used as part of management information to improve and develop staff practices. The young person we have already mentioned, Billy, was frequently restrained by staff during his time in secure accommodation. Staff became tired, both physically and emotionally, of having to deal with him in what time after time developed into physical confrontations. The debriefing sessions, which were put in place as a specific aspect of his management plan, were intended to provide staff with opportunities to let off steam but also to try to think about whether or not they had been able to implement agreed strategies about responding to Billy's behaviour. It is important in debriefing to avoid staff feeling that they are being persecuted about how they behaved in what they have experienced as a difficult and stressful situation. Achieving this depends on the wider culture of the organisation being one that is supportive towards staff but also one in which it is possible to look at what went wrong and why in a way that promotes good practice and is healthily critical of bad.

Focusing on the use of physical restraint raises a number of acute questions about aspects of work in secure units. For some the question may need to be asked as to whether or not it is ever justifiable to use methods of physical control with young people. Experience would suggest that to preclude their use would not be a viable option and that there are circumstances in which, in order to maintain safety, staff need to be confident and well-organised enough to intervene physically. Establishing adequate models for resolving conflict depends on there being an organisation-wide agreement about basic values which apply throughout and which must include the assumption that all individuals can expect to be treated with respect. If these values are to be made real in the life of a secure unit, then it is essential that the culture of that organisation at every level supports staff in their efforts to work positively with young people and to model and practise with them alternative approaches to resolving problems and conflicts. However, it is also essential that staff know that they will be supported by their immediate and senior managers if they have responded appropriately to a serious conflict situation and used proper professional judgement in the application of the approved techniques of physical restraint. Over recent years there has been a steady erosion in belief amongst residential social work staff about how reliable this support is likely to be, and this has had dangerous consequences as staff have been left uncertain about how they should act. In a difficult situation, requiring a firm response, it is equally inappropriate for staff either to intervene hesitantly or to retreat, as both reactions increase the likelihood of a member of staff or a young person getting hurt. The ambivalence that staff feel in these situations reflects the wider ambivalence we have already noted about the whole purpose and role of secure units. There is also the fact that society in general has become increasingly ambivalent about the nature and meaning of authority and in particular about how adults should exercise authority over children and young people. This ambivalence resonates throughout all systems and institutions dealing with young people but is most sharply focused by the issues that arise in secure units. The mixture of staff feeling unsupported and their managers fearing the repercussions from external management or from pressure groups is a poisonous brew that does no one any good, least of all young people. When asked to venture their opinions about how they want their residential unit to be, and how they want staff to behave towards them, young people are clear that they prefer staff who are confident and able to exercise proper authority when the need arises. In one secure establishment staff undertook an exercise to work with the young people to draw up a list of ground rules to which staff and young people could subscribe and which would shape the behaviour of everyone in the unit. By far and away the most desired feature for the young people in the group was that the unit should be safe and that this safety should be protected by the staff. Where the values of respect and trust are at the fore and evident in the structures and routines of a unit, then the management of difficult behaviour, even when the use of physical control is required, is much more readily acceptable to young people. In such circumstances they will feel that it is ultimately their safety and welfare that are being guarded.

Responding to complaints and allegations

Much good work has been done over recent years in developing a healthier climate in residential work with children and young people and this has included a recognition of the need for clear and effective complaints procedures to be in place and to be used. All secure units are required to have complaints procedures which can be accessed by young people and provide a vehicle for them to challenge any aspect of their care or management. Young people, however, require a great deal of encouragement to develop the confidence and trust to use formal procedures for airing their concerns and views. They often benefit from the support provided by one of the several sources of independent advocacy which now provide services to secure units and whose staff can advise and help young people in these matters. A healthy approach in a secure unit is to provide regular forums for young people to share with staff in discussing issues about the life of the unit and identifying any ways in which this might be improved. When these opportunities exist and young people can see that their concerns are taken seriously, this makes it easier both for relatively small matters to be resolved and also it creates a climate within which a young person is likely to feel that it is safe to raise a more serious issue. One of the difficulties that frequently arises is that what a young person considers 'serious' may not be so regarded in the view of a staff team. As well as remembering that sometimes when a young person raises an apparently trivial matter they are in fact trying to communicate about something more serious, the point remains, as with so much in residential settings, that what is a small detail to one person or group of people is a big deal to another. The way in which these apparently small matters are resolved actually tells as much about the real values of a secure unit as the way in which larger issues and problems are dealt with.

> Tracy complained loudly and heatedly to staff that a small doll which she had been allowed to keep in her room had been

touched by staff who had been doing some tidying up in her room. Tracy had a real problem not only with keeping her room tidy but also in her own attention to personal hygiene, so that for staff to be close to her and work with her around these issues was demanding. In the context of priorities about what was important the touching of a small doll did not rank particularly highly. However, the degree of Tracy's complaints and the threats that accompanied them put this issue to the top of the agenda in the unit for quite a long time. It was only as a result of staff spending time with Tracy and trying to talk to her about what was going on that it was revealed that the doll had been bought for her by her mother on the only occasion when she had remembered her daughter's birthday, and from this came a whole lot of material about the relationship between Tracy and her mother and the feelings that Tracy carried about her mother's lack of care and attention to the needs of her daughter.

One of the most contentious and distressing situations that can arise in a secure unit is when a young person makes a complaint about the behaviour of a member of staff. Responding to this situation entails a number of judgements being made about the nature of the complaint and a sensitive and alert management team who are able to pick out from what is being said the pointers which indicate the seriousness of the issue. At some point a complaint, 'Mr X shouted at me unfairly', becomes an allegation, 'Mr X hit me.' It is when an allegation centres on the direct behaviour of staff towards a young person and particularly when it is about an alleged assault or act of sexual misconduct that anxiety levels go through the roof in both the staff and young people's groups and a serious conflict situation has to be confronted within the unit.

Why does a young person make this kind of allegation? The most obvious answer is because it is true and a member of staff has stepped over the boundary and breached the trust placed in them. In residential settings when a young person makes an allegation against a member of staff a tension is almost instantly created between two extremes of response: those which at once assume that a young person is telling the truth and the member of staff is guilty of at least something; and those which side with the member of staff to protect them from the effects of being falsely accused. If either of these stances is uncritically adopted, then whatever the underlying conflict may be becomes heightened and the different per-spectives about the substance of the issue are polarised. In some situa-tions there is not much doubt about what actually happened and, provided those concerned are prepared to be straightforward and honest about the events, then a resolution can be reached. It is those qualities of honesty and straightforwardness, however, that are not always easily found when feelings are running high and both adults and young people are extremely anxious about what may be going to happen to them. It is generally the case that, whatever the circumstances, a member of staff involved in an allegation feels vulnerable and often guilty even when they have not done anything wrong. This level of feeling should never be underestimated for the member of staff concerned because if a young person does make a false allegation its effect can be devastating.

In making an allegation a young person may be attempting to exercise some control or power in a situation in which they have little of either, and by so doing can let adults know about something that is troubling them. Sometimes, however, feelings of vulnerability and isolation occa-sioned by being locked up in a secure unit become confused with memo-ries of what has happened in the past and a young person projects these into their current relationship with a particular member of the adult staff group. A young person's power in making an allegation is increased if the organisational response is to immediately suspend the member of staff concerned. As the adult is immediately seen to 'disappear' off the unit, the popular view about the truth of the allegation appears to be confirmed. Staff's feelings of helplessness are often compounded in these situations as although there may clearly be no substance to the allegation, and in due course they may be exonerated, in their view there is no redress. This may be an understandable reaction but it is an unhealthy one, and a staff group needs a good deal of support at this time to work through their initial re-actions and to think about what is going on and what meaning the experi-ence has for the young person. It is a mark of a mature staff group and of a well-established unit when an incident like this can be openly talked about between staff and young people. Reactions to an allegation are also evident in the young people's group. Sometimes they become fiercely protective of the staff group and hostile towards the young person who makes an allegation. This can also be a two-edged sword, however, and should not just be taken by the staff group as a sign of support. The young people may in fact be more incensed about the amount of attention that has been given to another young person as a result of their having made an allegation, rather than about its substance. On the other hand, in a group of young people most of whom have themselves been abused, strong feelings are very easily stirred up when an allegation is in the air and they may adopt a strong anti-staff stance which affects all aspects of unit life for a while. It is at these times that the strength of the relationship between staff and management is tested out, and the young people are also very interested to see how the staff group as a whole reacts to the situation. For the young people there is a key question for which they are seeking an answer and an allegation provides an opportunity to ask it again: 'Do you believe me or do you believe the adult?' Of course such a question is most likely not just being asked about the here and now but is carrying a resonance from earlier abusive experiences and adult responses. There are young people who develop a pattern of making allegations and this can become very difficult for any residential unit to manage. One of the dangers in these circumstances is that attention may be diverted away from the underlying needs of the young person and institutional management needs come to dominate.

When a young person makes an allegation against a member of staff with whom they appear to have been developing a very close and supportive relationship this often comes as a surprise to both the individual and the staff team as a whole. In these circumstances a variety of reactions may be experienced from the member of staff concerned, including feelings of being let down and rejected, anger about all the apparently wasted time and energy they have put into the relationship, bewilderment, guilt and fear. The guilt experienced by the member of staff, who may actually start to feel like an abusing adult, comes from the powerfully projected feelings of the young person. As Professor Robert Young comments, such projections are aimed at finding a willing if unsuspecting target:

> When we project into another it is rather like fly-fishing: we cast something out that teases something out; it catches something there and brings it out. What we catch may have been swimming about minding its own business until our attention is caught by its lure ... the projection finds its Other and evokes (and usually exaggerates) something that was there but perhaps not virulently so.
>
> (Young 1995)

Relationships established by individual key workers and personal officers with a young person may become particularly intense. Although such closeness is potentially beneficial for a young person there are occasions when it becomes too much for them to tolerate, and making an allegation is a way of defending against their fear of intimacy and what it might mean or how it might end. Although an allegation of this sort does take everyone by surprise, a good system of staff support and supervision should at least be able to prepare for such an eventuality, even if it cannot predict it.

> Alan was a 15-year-old young man sentenced to three years for a series of burglaries from the homes of elderly people. He had a long history of antisocial behaviours which included difficulties in making relationships with other children and in turn fighting and bullying them. He had been disruptive at school which resulted in his being suspended and finally ex-pelled. Early on in his life Alan's family had sought help from social services and he was placed in a number of children's homes and foster care placements, all of which had been un-able to contain or to manage him and from which on several occasions he had been removed after making unsubstantiated allegations against carers. Alan had a very low concentration span which made it difficult for him to settle at any activity for more than a very brief period. He had been seen by a number of child psychiatrists who diagnosed conduct disorder. On admission to a Young Offender Institution Alan went into a spiral of antisocial behaviours. Despite the best efforts of staff Alan could not settle into activities or education. He pro-voked other young people, calling them names and winding them up to the extent that he was regularly assaulted and had to be protected by staff. He would also bully those more vul-nerable than himself and increasingly he spent long periods of time alone in his cell, on the hospital wing or in the segrega-tion unit. What made his management even more difficult was that on those occasions when staff had to intervene, either to rescue Alan from his peers or to prevent him from hurting another young person, he would make an allegation that he was being victimised, bullied by staff or physically assaulted. His allegations also extended to times when he was in the segregation unit or on the hospital wing. These behaviours became a recurring pattern and added enormously to the staff's feelings of being absolutely drained by having to look after Alan and by the difficulties of keeping both him and others around him safe.

In thinking about Alan the allegations did seem to be a way of causing further disruption and of exercising some power in a situation in which he clearly felt vulnerable. His problems were long-standing and had not been much improved by the interventions which had been tried prior to custody. In many ways the large institution and its routines only served to make matters worse, as Alan was exposed to a highly stimulating environment and expected to relate to large groups of people which he found stressful. Trying to sort out whether or in what ways Alan had been treated badly proved almost impossible when so much was going on at the same time, and both staff and other young people were becoming increasingly frustrated by his continual demands and disruptive behaviour. In the end Alan was transferred to another establishment and this was repeated several times during the course of his sentence as the same problems recurred in each setting. Alan was failed in that none of his placements was able to create a sufficiently containing structure around him which would have allowed for some space to be created to think about the nature of his problems from a longer-term perspective and to implement a short-term management plan. The failure to achieve this was partly due to a lack of resources preventing time being spent on one young person because of the needs of others, but it was also due to the way in which institutional responses to Alan's behaviour, and in particular his allegations against staff, prevented any thinking taking place and served to increase the pressure to move him on to another placement.

The following example illustrates the way in which a particularly intense key worker relationship can fuel an allegation by a young person against a member of staff with whom they have appeared to establish a close working relationship. John was just 15 years old when he was sentenced to two years' custody for an indecent assault on a younger boy who lived near by in the neighbourhood. John had not been attending school and his family had raised concerns with social services about how he was spending time away from home, and there were suspicions that he was acting as a prostitute for older men.

Initially John appeared to settle in the secure unit and to develop a close relationship with his male key worker with whom he shared a number of interests and activities. John was not a popular member of the peer group and the young men in particular found him odd and quarrelsome. Issues of sexuality are always close to the surface in work with adolescents and, partly as a result of his presentation, John was subject to much speculation from the other young males about whether or not he was gay, although they were not so subtle in their approach to this question. He would react to this by behaving in an exaggerated 'camp' style and would 'borrow' clothing from the girls to dress up in around the unit, which provoked even greater hostility. The girls liked John and his company and he became something of a pet within their group. John's general behaviour was compliant although there were two incidents in which he lost his temper and on one occasion he threw a cup of hot water towards a member of staff. Staff attitudes towards John were mixed. Some of the male staff found him very difficult and uncomfortable to be around, whilst on the whole the women liked him, although there were a couple of the female staff who also felt very uneasy about him. John's key worker had a good relationship with him although he was quite challenged by the issue of John's sexuality and in what way, if at all, this could be talked about. Issues came to a head when the rest of the young people's group found out the offence for which John had received his custodial sentence. It was never clear how this information came into the group but the young people, and in particular the boys, protested absolute horror at John's offence, although in reality they were terrified at the way in which it confronted them directly with their own dilemmas about developing sexuality. On occasions this fear turned to direct attacks on John, but for most of the time it was the staff who had to bear the brunt of their confusion and anger. During this time John was also becoming more and more hostile towards his key worker who tried to maintain some link with him although he was finding the issues very difficult to come to terms with. It was in this context that John made an allegation that his key worker had sexually abused him. This was devastating to the member of staff and fuel to the fire for the rest of the staff team and also for the young people. The allegation had to be investigated and whilst this was happening the key worker was suspended from work. The rest of the staff team were furious at what was happening and were requesting John's immediate removal from the secure unit. The young people were also angry at the allegation and became vociferously supportive of the staff position. In the end the allegation was found to be unsubstantiated, but John's place in the unit could not be sustained and he was transferred to another unit for the remainder of his sentence.

This was an unusual set of circumstances and events but they illustrate how highly charged issues can overtake a residential unit through the acting out of just one of its residents. The allegation seemed on reflection to be a way in which John could distance himself from the staff group, and from his key worker in particular, and thus avoid the painful work of having to resolve what appeared to him to be an overwhelmingly difficult life situation.

As we have seen, dealing with allegations involves complex processes in which extreme positions must be avoided. Resolving these situations is never only an administrative exercise and neither a mechanistic use of procedures nor a failure to confront issues relating to the presenting needs of the young person gives sufficient respect to the integrity of the adults and young people involved. Understanding the implications of these processes for staff, young people and the unit as a whole should not only play a large part in the way managers approach the task of offering support to those involved, but also inform the way in which the investigation of the substance of allegations proceeds. Investigation is crucial because the allegations may be true, in which case to have appeared not to have believed them or to attempt to minimise their seriousness will only serve to increase a young person's own feelings of worthlessness as an object of abuse. However, it is essential that the thinking and investigating that are demanded in these situations are boundaried within a transparent and known procedural framework which sets out how young people and staff will be listened to and supported. As when dealing with incidents involving physical restraint it must be made explicit in the values of the secure unit that everyone has the right to be protected from any form of abuse of power and that the safety and security of individuals are a paramount responsibility. If the processes for managing investigations and resolving issues arising from allegations have to be crystal-clear, then the mechanisms for announcing the outcomes to both staff and young people have to be equally translucent. Even when the conclusions are painful it is still the case that both adults and young people need to know what was done, why certain things happened and what the outcome of the investigation is. Secrets and lies are all too familiar to young people in secure units. This is why any suggestion of a cover-up or of not taking allegations seriously is highly destructive and almost certain to undermine ongoing relationships and any other type of therapeutic interventions.

From out of all the different situations we have discussed the importance of the role of staff shines clearly through. We have seen what a difficult area of work this is and the intense pressure that it can bring and the extreme anxieties it can provoke. The emphases of the issues raised in this chapter may all seem to beg the question, which is one I have found to be always worth asking potential new staff at interview: 'Why on earth do you want to do this job and why now?'

Chapter 6

What happens inside?
Part II

> Sentence structure and regimes programmes will deliver little unless the staff who establish and maintain the safe and secure environment, who are critically involved in a young person's personal development and in control of institutional routines, model consistently positive attitudes and behaviours. The establishment of good relationships with young people is an essential part of encouraging their personal development.
>
> (Prison Service Order 4950: 3.3.1)

Most adults coming into residential work are motivated by a genuine desire to do something positive which will be of help to children and young people. Although these adults may have had only limited previous experience they must be attracted to the prospect of working with young people. In future this is also likely to be a requirement for the recruitment of prison officers, who will increasingly be selected for the specific purpose of working with the group of young people in custody who are under the age of 18 years. One of the aims of a good induction and initial training programme is to harness this early raw enthusiasm and underpin it with a knowledge and skill base upon which staff can go on to develop sound professional practices. Enthusiasm and a desire to help young people are essential prerequisites for this kind of work, although they are not sufficient in themselves. However, an important question to ask staff, whose core work is the day-to-day care and management of young people and who have a very important role to play in the delivery of intervention programmes, is also a very simple one: 'Do you like young people?' There is also another part to the question: 'Do young people like you?' Sometimes there are different answers to these questions and if that is the case then there are some further questions to be asked in supervision.

The importance of residential staff in ensuring the reliable and consistent delivery of the daily routines and in maintaining a safe environment for young people and staff cannot be overestimated. To do this work successfully requires a very tricky combination of personal qualities and inter-personal skills, which are supported by a set of sound professional values and informed by a well-understood body of knowledge about child and adolescent development and behaviour. This is a blend that is very hard to teach in formal courses or for students to learn in standard approaches to training. Although there is an increasing recognition of the central importance of this aspect of the work of staff – which is contemporaneously described by such terms as 'pro-social modelling' or being a 'significant adult' – there is little by way of more detailed explorations into what these roles actually demand of staff in the performance of their day-to-day duties. We have already looked at some of the pressures that are placed upon staff and some of the negative ways in which these pressures are defended against at both an institutional and an individual level. Part of the way of guarding against defensive attitudes and behaviours is to provide for staff a model in which they can see how positive attitudes and behaviours significantly influence the young people in their care. In a very useful summary about the needs of young people in custody, which they draw from two of their Thematic Reviews, *Young Prisoners* (1997) and *Suicide is Everyone's Concern* (1999), the Prison Service Inspectorate are explicit that:

> the qualities required by staff working with young people in custody must include fairness, sensitivity, patience, resilience, eagerness to work with young people, willingness to listen and learn, enthusiasm for teamwork, preparedness to take responsibility, to be comfortable as role models and, above all, a sense of humour.
>
> (HM Inspectorate of Prisons 1999)

The relationships that staff develop with young people in a secure unit are not formed in a vacuum but in the context of the day-to-day life of the residential unit and through participation in the ordinary routines that make up that life. The focus for these tasks is such ordinary and mundane matters as getting up in the morning, meal times, social and recreational activities and going to bed. Although there is a range of other tasks in which residential staff may become involved and which are also very important – such as supporting a young person in education, facilitating family contacts and co-working in programmes – it is the routine tasks with which they are most concerned. However, both the routine and more specialist activities are the vehicles through which staff influence and impact on young people. How staff behave in all of these activities, and the way in which the personal qualities they possess become apparent in their dealings with the young people, are the real tests for the effectiveness of pro-social role modelling, for becoming a significant adult in the life of a young person and, at least in part, for shaping their personal development.

Pro-social role modelling

Pro-social role modelling is not only about behaviour, it is also inextricably linked to language. Listening to how staff speak to young people and to what they say provides a number of clues about underlying values in a secure unit and how the staff group perceives the young people living there. Traditional prison service language and terminology have come under particular scrutiny in relation to their appropriateness for describing aspects of the new regimes for under 18-year-olds. References to young people as 'inmates', to meal times as 'feeding', to rooms as 'cells', or to time spent by young people in their rooms as 'bang up' have all been challenged as to their suitability. A change of terminology does not in itself guarantee a change in underlying assumptions associated with its use, but it is a beginning. Some of these language changes have been assisted by the way in which the prison service is now required to function as part of a wider secure estate and to work in multi-agency arrangements with Youth Offending Teams. Since the inception of the Youth Justice Board, work with young offenders has developed a discrete vocabulary which all agencies have to incorporate into their discourse in order to be seen as credible partners in the system. However, it is within institutions that the greatest changes need to occur and it will take time before the words and phrases used are truly expressive of the values they are meant to communicate. This is not an exercise in political correctness but a recognition of the power of words in conveying meaning and of the significance of their impact at all levels. The way a message is delivered determines how it is received and is as important as the content itself. Use of sarcasm or a belittling nickname are ways in which staff can very easily abuse their power and humiliate a young person. A barked instruction, even if preceded by a 'please', is less likely to convey a sense of respect than a polite request addressed in a clear and firm manner.

The importance of daily routines

Arriving at a secure unit

Language and behaviour come together for staff in their performance of the key routines which make up much of life in a secure unit. One of the problems for staff working in residential settings, and secure units are no exception, is to keep their understanding of the importance of these daily routines fresh and at the front of their minds on each occasion that they perform the tasks. This is a difficult principle to maintain and in order to do so it is essential that the value of the tasks and of the staff carrying them out is fully and explicitly recognised. If this is not achieved then staff lose their motivation and the routines become stale and the important significance that they carry becomes lost. Nowhere is this more important than at the time when a young person is received into a secure unit and inducted into its routines and daily activities. Experience shows that the manner in which a young person is received into an establishment and how their first impressions are shaped by the way staff induct them on to a unit have a direct bearing on their later achievements in custody. Many young people arrive at secure units tired and hungry after a long journey, confused about where they are and frightened at the unknown possibilities that await them. The only information they may have is what they have gleaned from the horror stories they have been told by their mates outside. For staff there is a difficult balance to achieve between ensuring that the necessary paper work and administrative tasks are completed properly and ensuring that individual care and attention are given to the needs of the young person about whom they may know very little. Making assessments at this time as to the potential vulnerability of a young person, and their propensity for self-harm or for being aggressive towards others, is a skilled task and should be regarded as the priority. The first stage of the admission process is completed by taking the young person to their living unit, introducing them to the staff on the unit and handing over as much information as possible. Sometimes it is the same staff who are present at the initial admission who work with the young people on the living units. In larger establishments this is not necessarily the case and therefore it is even more important that continuity is achieved between the different staff groups involved and that information collated in one area is transferred with the young person to another. From then on it becomes the unit staff's responsibility to settle a young person into the living unit, introduce them to other young people and provide them with clear expectations about what is required and what is going to happen next.

Morning routines

Getting young people up in the morning and ensuring that they manage to wash and tidy their room before coming to breakfast are important routines which have meaning at several different levels. Most straightforwardly the routine is helping to establish good personal habits that it is hoped will be continued on release when the young person will have to get up to go to school or work. At the same time a high standard of order and cleanliness is being maintained on the living unit which supports young people in developing a generally positive attitude towards themselves and each other. Even at these levels, however, there are different ways in which the routine may be carried out, which range from a loud issuing of general instructions to the whole group accompanied by a ritual jangling of keys and banging of doors, to a more individually thought out process in which each young person is woken and prepared for the coming day's activities. The latter approach is likely to be informed by an understanding of how at the moment of the first call the member of staff is going into the personal space of a young person at a point where they are coming from sleep into wakefulness and perhaps emerging from a troubled night of disturbing dreams. Managing this routine in a sensitive and non-intrusive manner so that a young person is enabled to see that they have been acknowledged and respected but which at the same time achieves the task is skilled work. It requires staff to know something about what night-times may mean to disturbed young people, apply this to the individuals in their care and be able to use a range of skills to deal with whatever reactions they receive from a young person, whilst at the same time achieving their purpose, i.e. having the group up and eating breakfast within a specified time period. Resources play a part in this. If there are two staff to wake thirty or so young people then the level of personal contact is likely to be limited. This is why staffing levels is an important topic and why discussions of the type 'how many staff do you really need?' must be informed by a thoughtful understanding of the nature of the task and the needs of young people rather than by the application of some mathematical formula devised for other settings and purposes. The way young people are woken up to begin the day makes an important contribution to their sense of being contained and looked after. It is also likely to have an important bearing on how the rest of the day goes and what degree of success is achieved in the activities it brings. In this respect it is useful to compare the morning routine to the admissions process, as in a sense each morning's routine is a re-enacting of that initial reception to the secure unit.

Night-times

The same issues arise in thinking about night-time routines and the ways in which staff approach the task of helping young people to make the transition from activity to sleep. Planning the evening routine so that a general slowing down of the pace of the day is progressed to the point where every young person is in their room and prepared for sleep is an important task for a staff team. It is one in which all members of the team need to make a particular contribution by using their individual personal qualities and repertoire of skills. The way in which staff leave the unit at the end of the evening shift is also worth thinking about. Boisterous farewells and laughter of relief at being off duty or loudly made arrangements as to which pub everyone is going to meet up in are not likely to help settle an anxious group of young people for whom the experience of being locked up in a small single room may well exacerbate past fears and increase their sense of abandonment. Young people do not necessarily admit to the feelings being ascribed to them here. They may well join in the hearty farewells but almost certainly underneath even the most brash of exteriors there is going to be some underlying sadness and experience of loss each time this routine is enacted. Some young people are not so compliant and act out their distress at this time just in order to prevent staff from leaving. What is often dismissed as attention-seeking behaviour at night might be linked to some underlying anxiety, and more significantly it should also be remembered that dramatic acts of self-harm are more likely to occur at night. In effect what this means is that practice has to be re-thought every day, and whilst keeping these things in mind on every morning and night shift is hard, it is nevertheless an intrinsic part of the residential task.

Meals and the importance of food

Food plays a hugely important part in the provision of high-quality residential care. Well-prepared meals, served in adequate portions and to the taste of young people, are a basic necessity and satisfying this requirement contributes greatly to the overall smooth running of a residential unit. Giving young people the chance to prepare and cook food for themselves and others is a very practical way of developing living skills as well as encouraging a sense of doing something for other people which can give pleasure. Cooking also provides a positive activity for staff and young people to share in together and it provides a relaxed opportunity to do some talking at the same time. Meal times offer a number of different opportunities for staff to engage with young people. At a simple level they are social occasions at which staff and young people sit down and share what we hope is a pleasant experience. These are times when staff can talk naturally to young people and show an interest in what they have been doing. Asking about how a young person has got on in education or encouraging them to engage in some activity is a way of offering support and its relevance to a young person should not be underestimated. For many young people in secure units this kind of experience will not have been a feature of their earlier care from adults and so it can be an important learning opportunity for them. Staff, however, although aware of the occasion as a tool for developing a young person's social skills also need to be aware that a young person's reaction to the food which has been prepared for them may also be very telling about the nature and quality of their earlier care experiences.

The preparation, serving and eating of food inevitably arouse memories of the maternal care that a child has received. When a young person reacts to food with the complaint that 'this is shit', it is likely that they are saying something about how they have been cared for. They might also, of course, be saying something about how they are experiencing their immediate care and this is why it is so important that every meal time produces a consistently high quality of food and that staff are around to share the experience. It is also why it is wrong for staff to collude with derogatory remarks about the quality of the food even when it is unappetising. It is essential that those who prepare food in residential settings receive feedback about the meals for which they are responsible and are helped to understand the vital importance of their role in the kitchen and its significance for the young people in the unit. Staff groups too are generally very serious in their appreciation or otherwise of the food served and may, on occasions, use complaints about food served up to act out their feelings about not being listened to or cared for. It is interesting that in most prison service establishments staff do not share meals with the prisoners and it can be a disciplinary offence to be seen taking the prisoners' food. In most units looking after the younger populations, meal times are now communal events, although in some instances young people still have to collect their meals, take them to their room and eat them alone. These practices when applied to young people are not only lost opportunities for the furtherance of social skills training and the building of relationships but may also have unintended, psychologically damaging consequences as well. The preparation of food and its provision through meal times are important symbols of the nurture and care available in the setting. Well-planned and organised meal times, which are shared together by staff and young people, are further factors in creating an appropriately containing environment in which everyone can feel safe and well looked after.

In between times

As well as playing a key role in the way primary care routines are delivered in the residential unit, staff must also be aware of the way in which their presence impacts on young people at those times 'between' events and activities. In secure units the way in which leisure time or social recreation is structured varies. In local authority secure units or secure training centres staff actively engage with young people in a wide range of activities. During these periods there are many opportunities for social learning to take place and for staff to work with young people through their participation in an activity. In Young Offender Institutions these periods are known as 'Association' and, partly as a result of significantly lower staffing numbers on duty at any one time, young people tend to be left to their own devices, with staff standing on one side watching and monitoring. As with the main care routines in prison service establishments this represents wasted opportunities for staff to have contact with the young people in a way that can bring benefits to the life of the unit as a whole.

The role of staff

The way in which staff behave and speak to young people is, as we have described, a critical determinant of the overall experience for a young person during their time in a secure unit. The ability of a member of staff to relate well to young people, the ability to offer them encouragement and positive praise for the efforts they make, and the ability to have a good understanding not only of the importance of carrying out routines, but of their underlying significance for each young person, are important indicators of their suitability for this work. There is really no clear-cut blueprint for how to do this work but there are certainly some traps into which staff can easily fall in their attempts to relate well to young people. We have already discussed the extreme dangers of being too distant or over-involved, which are perhaps the most obvious mistakes for inexperienced staff. Trying to be a 'mate' is also another potential pitfall, as is the use of street language or indeed swearing as a way of seeking to gain some credibility. It is also not helpful to be the kind of member of staff who is 'too' earnest or serious. A sense of humour has already been identified as an indispensable quality. Young people do not want to be 'therapied' all the time. Some never do! Knowing when to intervene and when to back off and give a young person some needed space and time is part of the repertoire of skills that members of staff need to develop. When staff are observed pursuing a young person, desperate to 'get them to talk', it can be useful to ask the question, for whose benefit is this? Residential staff who are over-anxious to become counsellors and think that a secure unit gives them a captive client group are bad news! Being sensitive to the fine tuning that is needed to decide the most appropriate response in any given situation comes from experience. This is why the role of first line managers is so important and one to which we shall return, for if young people can get something positive from forming a relationship with a significant adult so too can a new and inexperienced member of the staff team.

Another useful way of thinking about what staff have to do to fulfil the role of a significant adult is to look at the wide range of roles that they are actually called upon to perform in their daily duties. In one unit the team were asked to undertake an exercise in which they had to identify and define the roles they recognised themselves taking during the course of a shift. The exercise had to stop when they reached over a hundred! Included within the list were: mum, dad, brother, sister, teacher, friend, counsellor, advisor, servant and so on. Many of these responses were expressions of how the young people regarded the adult staff team, and reflected the powerful projections which, as we have already seen, emerge from the complex matrix of relationships that exists between and within different groups. To develop a clear model of what a significant adult should be and how they might behave in a range of situations, each member of staff needs a sufficient personal maturity and a good degree of personal confidence and self-awareness. Such qualities can then be used to assist them to understand more about the contexts in which their relationships with young people are formed and to think about the ways in which the different roles they are called upon to play impinge upon them in the course of their daily work.

We have focused our discussion about the role of care staff and prison officers on their routine day-to-day work with young people on the living unit. The relationships that they form in this context, however, can be a useful basis for supporting a young person in their involvement with more formal programmes and in more structured individual work as a key worker or personal officer. Increasingly staff are being encouraged to take on these roles and to participate in group work programmes tackling offending behaviour, or to contribute to casework planning and report writing. This is a wholly right-minded development as it acknowledges the particular strengths of the relationships that care staff and prison officers may establish with young people and the potential for those relationships to impact directly on a young person during their time in custody. It is also a recognition that through these relationships and in the day-to-day interactions of staff and young people on the residential unit a great deal of information and material can be collated about the needs of each young person and the nature of their problems and difficulties. To perform these particular roles an additional level of training is necessary in order for staff to acquire the specialist knowledge that they need and to develop the increased range of skills that they have to employ. Although the addition of this dimension to the job is undoubtedly beneficial for all concerned, working as a personal officer or key worker can sometimes be too much for newer staff who are still struggling to come to terms with the challenges of their job at the day-to-day level which is complex enough. A planned and careful progression to assuming key-working or personal officer responsibilities is essential. For this to be achieved, a consistent management approach has to be taken with regard to the professional development of staff, which encompasses a clear definition of the kind of tasks they are required to perform at every stage.

Regime ingredients for a 'healthy' secure environment

During the course of his tenure as Chief Inspector of Prisons, Sir David Ramsbotham developed a model for his inspections which included the concept of 'healthy prisons'. There are a number of features of this model which must all be satisfied if an establishment is to be deemed healthy: the weakest prisoners must feel safe; prisoners must be treated with respect as individuals; prisoners must be fully and purposefully occupied; and opportunities must be provided for prisoners' links with families to be strengthened. These are the basic requirements in achieving the aims of the prison service, which are to keep prisoners safely in custody and prepare them for release in a way that means they are less likely to re-offend. They are also fundamental requirements in the development of regimes for young people in custody, and each has a particular application in reference to meeting the needs of this particular group. In expanding the criteria with regard to young people the key regime ingredients must include and emphasise: a safe and secure environment; a multi-disciplinary and multi-agency approach to casework planning; individually focused programmes; education and training; health care; and family contacts.

Although mainly a prison service term, 'regime' is more and more being used to describe the way in which all aspects of life and work in secure units are organised, managed and delivered. We have emphasised the consistent and reliable provision of daily routines as an essential part of the framework for life in a secure unit, and the key role that staff play in ensuring their effective delivery. These routine activities and the way in which they are carried out by staff are critical in ensuring that the secure unit provides a safe and secure environment for adults and young people alike. A staff group who have knowledge of the individual young people living in the unit are equipped to identify potential problems as they arise and to intervene quickly to prevent incidents occurring. In particular this knowledge allows staff to spot changes in young people's moods and to think about possible reasons for this and what might be done by way of response. It also means that staff are more alert to the presence of bullies in the group and can be sensitive to any undertones of racial abuse. This personal knowledge and attention to the individual needs of the young people is a large element in the process of containment which we have previously discussed with regard to maintaining safety and security.

Physical security

There are, however, wider institutional policies and procedures which need to be in place to support the efforts of staff and young people in maintaining a healthy and safe environment. This includes making sure that the physical security of the building is monitored and that young people are kept within the unit. How this is achieved varies between establishments and depends to a large extent on the age and design of the buildings. More important is the way staff carry out the procedures that are in place to maintain this security and how intrusive they are allowed to become in the day-to-day life of the community inside the unit. Similar consideration needs to be given to other security procedures such as the way searches are conducted of both those inside the institution and people who are visiting. Often these procedures are mechanistic and carried out as rituals, with the reasons for their implementation apparently forgotten. As with primary care routines it is necessary to maintain a freshness in staff's approach to these security routines and to understand the underlying reasons for them. Searching a visitor, a young person or indeed members of staff is by definition an intrusive act and can be used to emphasise the differences in the power relationship that exists between searcher and searched in a negative or indeed a bullying way.

Unless illicit substances or dangerous articles are prevented from entering a unit, the environment will not be safe and secure. The need to carry out vigilant searches to ensure that this remains the case is likely to be understood by all, particularly if they can see that it is for their protection that staff are acting. It is also likely to be more acceptable if the search is done in a way that preserves respect for the individual and with a clear rationale given for its necessity.

Anti-bullying and anti-racist policies and practice

All secure units must have a clear anti-bullying strategy in operation that is effective in identifying bullying and in dealing with situations as they arise. Key elements of such a strategy include:

- The prominent promotion across the unit of the core basic value that bullying will not be tolerated, and the nomination of an actively committed senior member of staff to champion the implementation of the policy.
- Every person in the establishment being strongly encouraged to sign up to this value, and supporting this in the design of key regime instruments such as the incentives and privileges scheme.
- Examples of actual behaviours which are deemed bullying being included in the definition and ensuring that these are agreed and known about by all staff and young people coming into the unit.
- Staff being prepared to challenge bullying behaviours as they occur and making sure that their own behaviour models and demonstrates alternative ways of how people should relate to each other.
- Providing support to those young people who are the victims of bullying and ensuring that opportunities are made available for them to safely share their concerns with staff.
- Undertaking remedial work with those who behave in a bullying fashion.
- Having in place systems to regularly review the effectiveness of the policy and its implementation.

A similar set of values and procedures should be clearly in place to combat racist attitudes and behaviours as they occur within an establishment, and there should be a similarly high profile given to ensuring that the policy is known and procedures are followed when necessary.

Incentive schemes

An effective incentives and privileges scheme also contributes to maintaining a safe and secure environment. Whatever the details of a particular scheme they are an important tool for staff to be able to use in their work with young people. The effectiveness of these schemes is greatly enhanced in a setting where there are already strong and positive relationships between staff and young people. They are not a substitute for good relationships and the value that these have for young people but they are a means by which staff can give tangible and positive reinforcement to the progress being achieved by a young person. An incentives and privileges scheme is not an instrument that should just be applied irrespective of the individual needs of the young people in the group. Of course such schemes have a place in marking out some basic rules and expectations in a unit about what are acceptable and unacceptable sorts of behaviour. They are most effective, however, if the achieving of rewards is not just dependent upon a young person attaining an acceptable level of institutional behaviour but if rewards are gained as a result of real progress being made within a designated individual programme. Such a programme may be focused on specific behavioural change or active participation in a particular educational course or a series of sessions tackling offending behaviour. Although the relatively short periods of time that most young people spend in a secure unit inevitably mean that the staff have to take the greater degree of responsibility for establishing and maintaining the unit's culture and ethos, the role of the young people themselves in contributing to this should not be underestimated. Rewarding young people for contributing to the development of a positive culture amongst their own peer group and encouraging them to take responsibility for what goes on in a unit is a powerful way of reinforcing the development of pro-social behaviour and of providing good experiences of living alongside other people. As we saw in the last chapter, this is more likely to occur in a setting in which the importance of relationships is emphasised and in which staff are pro-active in engaging the young people and in providing opportunities for feedback to be given to both individuals and the group as a whole.

Group meetings

A common feature of many of the young people who are placed in secure units is that they are seemingly oblivious of the impact that their behaviour has on those around them. Regular discussions about this issue with examples given from the here and now of unit life, linked to the consequences of antisocial behaviours being immediately reflected in the rewards scheme, is a very effective way of impacting upon young people. If a routine of daily or weekly meetings is established for the purposes described above, then it can be highly illuminating to allow the young people to take responsibility for chairing the meetings and to encourage maximum participation by all members of the group. Not only does this foster the sense of young people taking increased responsibility for what goes on in the unit but it yields important information about how an individual young person is viewed by the rest of the group. In addition, careful observation of the general interactions within the group reveals a lot about the current mood and state of the unit. Group meetings are a particularly effective way of confronting a group of young people about the respective roles that they play in group life. A common and worrying problem amongst groups of young people in residential settings is the scapegoating that goes on with certain individuals. Scapegoating is similar to the phenomenon whereby individual staff members are targeted, but in the young people's group there may also be issues of bullying to consider, as well as trying to determine what it is about a young person that seems to invite a negative reaction from peers. Staff are very familiar with the problems of the young person who is a perpetual victim, who everyone seems to have it in for and for whom staff find themselves feeling little sympathy. In these circumstances it is not just the group who must be challenged about their reactions. Work is needed with the individual to try to increase their awareness of the reaction they are causing, and with staff to help them understand something about the meaning of the victim's behaviour so that they may begin to think about how to manage the situation as a whole. In these situations staff often appeal to the widely held myth of residential work that if only so-and-so wasn't here then the rest of the group would be so much easier to manage and would do so much better.

A bit like Billy, Danny was continually provoking the anger and frustration of his peers but in his case he repeatedly demanded that staff protect him from the other young people on the living unit. Unfortunately for Danny, however, it was all too obvious to staff why the other young people sought him out, as Danny had the knack of being able to wind up the rest of the group not only by his behaviour but also by directing the most foul-mouthed comments at them. These usually included comments about their relationship to their mother and, as all those who work in secure units will know, there is an immediate and inevitable response to that phrase, which can be abbreviated to 'your mum', from the young people in the group. For staff it was increasingly frustrating trying to maintain the peace on the unit in circumstances where they had natural sympathy for the attackers or erstwhile bullies. Unlike Billy, however, Danny did have some capacity for thinking and for learning about himself and the effect he could have on others. A combination of consistent individual work with Danny, rehearsing other ways of gaining attention, and structuring individual time into his daily programme, together with consistently rewarding the rest of the group for ignoring Danny's more provocative behaviours, gradually reduced the number of incidents. All of this could be both talked about and modelled in the regular group meetings which took place on the living unit. This was also an opportunity for staff to learn about managing a difficult young person without recourse to scapegoating and insisting that Danny be transferred.

What should not be forgotten, especially by those who do not work routinely in these settings, is just how frustrating and tiring this work can be. Sometimes the dynamics of a group of young people seem completely impervious to any attempts at change, and individuals become stuck in roles with no indication of any possibility of change. When this occurs a staff team requires a great deal of support, as this is exactly the time when other issues of discontent surface and morale dips. There is no easy answer to any of this and it is only through perseverance and sheer professional determination that progress is likely to be made, if at all.

Involvement of families

One of the important outcomes of the research project, *Tell Them So They Listen*, is the finding that for young people in custody the links with their families and parents are of particular importance to them. Maintaining these links and even fostering and strengthening them is not easy when a young person is placed in a secure unit, perhaps many miles from their home. Most young people on release from a secure unit go home at some stage – if not straight away then later on. Staff can play an important role in supporting family contact for young people. Talking sensitively with them about their families, encouraging them to write and phone home regularly, ensuring that visits take place and being around at these times in order to meet family members are all worthwhile. Visiting times may be fraught but they are also real opportunities for staff to meet families, get to know them and find out more about the young person in their care. Often relationships within a family have been fractured by the events which led to a young person being placed in a secure unit, and in these cases staff can help build bridges between a young person and their family. Families are also intended to be an integral part of the casework system and should be invited to attend all case reviews, not just in a perfunctory way but personally and by emphasising the important role that they have to play. When families do attend the case reviews they should be made to feel that they are important contributors to the proceedings and that their views and those of the young person are being listened to and taken into account when planning for the future. In some secure units resources exist for more in-depth family work to take place, which can be of great benefit in helping the resettlement of a young person. However, even where this is not the case, it is still essential that the significance of family relationships is recognised and that basic arrangements are in place to support and encourage contact wherever possible. A number of secure units have regular family days when the families of young people placed in the unit are invited to come to the unit, meet staff and look at the work done by the young people. These events are very helpful in breaking down barriers and in supporting a young person, particularly when they are serving a long sentence in a secure unit.

> Terry was a young person who found it very difficult to settle into the routines of the secure unit having been sentenced to a very long term in custody for a serious and violent offence. His problems were exacerbated by the anxiety he felt about his mother, for whom prior to sentence he had been a main support at home, and also by her reaction to his sentence which resulted in her being antagonistic towards what she saw as the persecutory authority who had taken away her son – feelings which she projected towards the staff of the secure unit. Helping Terry to come to terms with his sentence and its long-term nature included some very close work with his mother to build up trust with her about the intentions of staff and the effect her behaviour was having on her son. Over a

period of time, through her visits and the way she was treated during her time on the unit, along with some practical help in making the arrangements for visiting the unit and in particular to attend the regular case review meetings, a better relationship was formed and both Terry and his mother began to work positively with the unit staff and with the assigned Youth Offending Team worker in the community.

Case review meetings – Training Plans

We noted in Chapter 2 how the structure of the Detention and Training Order demands close working between all agencies in the management of the sentence. The Training Plan, which is jointly developed by community and custodial agencies along with the involvement of the young person and their family, enshrines the aims and targets to be achieved during the course of the sentence. This plan is regularly reviewed by all the parties concerned with its implementation, and these reviews are a critical part of a young person's time in secure accommodation, acting as the co-ordinating thread which links the different parts of the regime in the secure unit and prepares the young person for their release into the community. The conduct of these meetings provides a valuable opportunity for professionals to model a consistent approach to the problems and needs of the young person, as well as to engage them and their family in the process of rehabilitation and in supporting the programme in the secure unit and outside. How things are presented in these meetings and how things are said about a young person are indicative of how a group of professionals are thinking about the young people in their care, and these are important occasions on which either a great deal of positive benefit can be gained or goodwill can easily be lost. For example, in the case of Terry and his mother, her attendance at reviews, and the support she received to enable her to attend, made life much better for the young person over the length of his sentence.

Offending behaviour programmes

We have constantly emphasised the importance of staff as pro-social role models for young people in the day-to-day routines and activities that make up life in a secure unit, and how the relationships established between adults and young people contribute significantly to the provision of a safe and secure environment. However, although these relationships have a therapeutic value in themselves they also serve to support and encourage a young person to engage in other important aspects of the regime. Although a great deal of learning goes on in routine activities there is also a place for a more focused approach to be taken to help young people to understand about the consequences of their delinquent behaviour and to acquire the necessary cognitive skills to avoid further offending. This is not an either/or choice as each element in a well-designed regime complements the other and provides material for the young person's overall experience.

The research base which provides the strongest foundation for the development of programmes for offenders is known as 'What Works'. Mainly developed with adult offenders in mind there is nevertheless a set of key principles which underpin all interventions of this type and which are equally applicable to an adolescent population. The main differences between adult and adolescent programmes tend to be in the areas of delivery style and the nature of the programme material. There are also issues about how much at any time can be effectively delivered to an adolescent group, and about the management of the group itself in terms of maintaining interest and focus. An effective programme based on 'What Works' principles must: have a sound theoretical base; link risk assessment to programme allocation; be responsive to individual learning styles; ensure a structured and directive approach; use cognitive behavioural methods; and maintain programme integrity. Hobbs and Hook, in a paper prepared for the Youth Justice Board, 'Research into Effective Practice with Young People in Secure Facilities', draw out a number of important conclusions to be considered when applying the principles of offending behaviour programmes to young offenders:

- Juveniles require a great deal of input in order to counteract other damaging influences to which they are susceptible.
- The relevance of pro-social role modelling to juveniles through the age range is important – the emphasis on providing tangible rewards and positive influences is particularly relevant to the developmental stage of juveniles.
- Pro-social modelling is an especially important and potentially powerful concept when applied to institutions ... an incarcerated young offender will be exposed to the characteristics of the institution in which they are held for the totality of their sentence, and the capacity for either a positive or negative effect is considerable.
- Work with young offenders needs to take account of their

developmental stage, the influence of peer group and the protective potential of education.

- Method and style of programme delivery must take into account the different learning styles of offenders. This will involve active, participatory methods. Materials and means of communication should be adjusted for use with young offenders.
- Programmes must recognise the breadth of offenders' problems and needs. Cognitive behavioural interventions will need to be supplemented by the practical acquisition of skills.
- Programme integrity: Programmes should be delivered consistently so that their impact can be evaluated.

(Hobbs and Hook Consulting 2000)

Despite the ever-increasing research and the sound principles that underpin it, offending behaviour programmes, and especially those being designed for young offenders, still have a number of unresolved issues at both theoretical and practical levels. More needs to be known about the relationship between the effectiveness of specific offending behaviour programmes and the impact that other elements of a custodial regime have on a young person's future offending behaviour. This is critical for the development of adequate models for regimes in secure units so that offending behaviour programmes, education and other specialist services can be fully integrated into a daily routine of activities and all members of staff can feel that they are contributing to the overall aim and purpose of the unit. One of the real difficulties in Young Offender Institutions is achieving a satisfactory balance between addressing and meeting the individual needs of each young person and at the same time maintaining the essential routines for group living. This is not just a resource issue but is directly linked to having a robust model of the nature of the task and the importance of each member of staff's role in delivering the overall regime experience. There is also a pressing need to develop specific offending behaviour programmes for young women. The differences in the offending patterns of young women and the particular needs that they present have begun to be recognised through the provision of different regime activities. The dynamics that arise through the interactions of staff and young people in a residential unit for young women have a particular quality to them, and staff working in this environment require specific support and training. More research is required in this area and there is still a great deal of work to be done to integrate specific programmes into a wider regime that has been designed specifically to meet the needs of young women serving a sentence in a secure unit.

A similar set of issues remains to be satisfactorily resolved with regard to meeting the explicit needs of young people from minority ethnic groups and ensuring that material used in the cognitive approaches taken in offending behaviour programmes is appropriate and relevant. In the same way there is clearly much to be done to engage more positively with the rich experiences that arise from the diverse family structures within these communities.

There are serious training implications in developing an integrated approach to work with young people in secure units and these have still not been fully thought through, let alone translated into training programmes or identified as required professional competencies. In addition it must be noted that at this time there is still a lack of specialist programmes for adolescent sex offenders, arsonists or those who commit violent offences including murder. Although these are a small minority of young offenders they present real challenges for management and treatment in secure units.

Educational provision

Many similar points may be made with regard to the provision of education services for young people in secure units as for offending behaviour programmes. Across the secure estate in local authority secure units, secure training centres and Young Offender Institutions there are many examples of excellent education programmes being offered to young people. However, these services are organised and delivered in establishments in a variety of ways which lead to inconsistencies in provision across the secure estate as a whole. In some settings the educational staff are directly employed by the secure unit, in others they are employed by the local education authority and seconded into the secure unit. The prison service currently operates a system whereby establishments contract out education services to their local colleges. This means that there are disparate levels of educational services provided in each establishment, resulting in wide variations in standards and no common range of curriculum opportunities for young people. This system also means that there is little flexibility available within establishments to address particular or immediate needs as they may arise.

The Youth Justice Board has at the top of its agenda the raising of educational standards for all young people in secure accommodation irrespective of the sector in which they are placed. This is linked to the increasing research evidence about the importance of education, training and employment opportunities in reducing offending rates amongst all categories of offenders including young people. The vision of the Youth Justice Board is that secure accommodation should embrace a model of Secure Colleges in which the emphasis on education is a priority.

> While the research base on the impact of different educational approaches on young offenders needs augmenting urgently, there are relevant findings. The most common finding of over 20 years of research is that people who participate in custodial education programmes are more likely to be employed and less likely to end up back in custody than non-participants. There is a growing body of research that disconnection from mainstream education and training is an extremely important risk factor for offending and reoffending .... The Detention and Training Order is a radical new sentence which challenges the traditional division between custodial and community interventions. The starting point for custodial interventions must be the intended outcomes for the entire Detention and Training Order. This implies that educational planning, monitoring of outcomes and the effective transition to education and training in the community must dominate the thinking of Young Offender Institutions from the moment of entry into custody.
>
> (Youth Justice Board, 2001)

The educational attainments of many of the young people entering custody are very low. A significant number of these young people have not attended school on a regular basis, sometimes for a period of several years. This lack of education is a tremendous disadvantage for young people and extremely damaging for their future life chances. On the other hand there are young people for whom a custodial sentence brings serious disruption to their education. Ensuring that these young people are able to continue with courses of study that they may already be pursuing is a responsibility not just for education services inside secure units but for the local education authority in the young person's home community. One of the main problems for all young people sentenced or remanded in custody is the disruption they experience with regard to whatever stable influence they may have had in the community. This might be school, family, social worker, youth worker or some other important contact. It is essential that in a young person's experience of custody this contact is not just maintained but strengthened through their individual programme. Building on current positives in the lives of young people and identifying and developing other strengths is an important part of the role of secure units. Providing a positive experience of education is a core task for secure units with young people of this age group. Much success is evident in those units that have developed education programmes that engage young people and offer them opportunities to catch up on missed years of schooling. Achieving in education is a tremendous way of boosting self-esteem and offers young people immediate chances for success to be recognised and accredited. Although it is sometimes said rather disparagingly that young people in secure units are a captive audience it is nevertheless always very impressive to see the kind of work that they produce in education and the level of formal achievement that is frequently attained.

Preparing young people for employment is another key feature for this age group and whilst opportunities for vocational training are available in many Young Offender Institutions their value is being increasingly recognised in other settings as well. Vocational training and the availability of opportunities to acquire a range of practical skills for the workplace has been a neglected area in recent years but the value of such courses is immense. The re-introduction of vocationally orientated courses into education provision for younger children from the age of 14 years is to be welcomed as they provide highly relevant opportunities for engaging the interest of young people. One of the main difficulties experienced by young people leaving secure units is maintaining their progress in education and continuing with a programme of studies in a school or college setting. Together with having stable accommodation the availability of continuing education, training or employment is a key factor in reducing further offending on release. More links are now being made between secure units and local education services and certainly the statutory requirement for education to be part of local Youth Offending Teams has done much to support this. A great deal of work is being done in this area by the Youth Justice Board who have identified education as a priority for their current planning. As other initiatives under the umbrella of Youth Support Services come on line, such as the Connexions Service, then, provided they can be properly integrated into the local Youth Offending Team services, there are likely to be ever-increasing opportunities for young people to maintain the progress which they often begin to make during their time in custody.

The Training Plan documentation for recording a young person's progress through their Detention and Training Order emphasises the central role that education should play both during the period in custody and also in the community phase of the sentence. Integrating this aspect of the programme into the whole experience of a young person in custody is not just the responsibility of education staff. Offering support to a young person, taking an interest in their education programme and encouraging them to succeed is a key role for prison officers and care staff. This daily support reflects no more than what a good parent does when they ask their child about how their day went at school. It may seem a small, ordinary thing but it is a very important part of building a young person's self-esteem and reinforcing in them the sense that they are of interest to those important adult figures in their lives during the period they are spending in custody.

Addressing mental health needs

As we noted in Chapter 2, the levels of psychiatric morbidity amongst young people in secure units are very high. It is therefore even more astonishing when just a cursory look at mental health services across the secure estate reveals a serious lack of resources and a repeat pattern of widely divergent service levels. Young people in secure units, however, have a wide range of general health needs and these are equally poorly provided for. It is the stated intention of the prison service that all people in prison establishments should expect to receive the same level and standard of health care as if they were in the community. To achieve this aim the management and delivery of health care services in prisons have become the responsibility of local health authorities, and each prison service establishment has been obliged to draw up an audit of the health care needs of their prisoners and provide an action plan for how these needs are best met and what resources are required. Young people have particular problems and it is important that as any structural changes in service provision are introduced the needs of the youngest population are adequately catered for. The situation is similarly difficult in local authority secure units where different arrangements for the provision of primary health care are in place from unit to unit. It is understandable in these instances that a busy local general practice does not want the problems that providing services to secure units may bring but it is unacceptable when these young people are denied proper access to medical care. Many young people coming into secure units have not attended to their basic health needs over several years and a period in custody can therefore be an opportunity to attend to routine matters such as visiting the dentist or optician. For most young people their immediate lifestyle prior to admission may well have had detrimental and damaging effects on their health. Some young people on admission to a secure unit require immediate treatment, and all of them require a longer-term approach to be taken with regard to education about lifestyle and healthy living. A great deal can be done in secure units to help young people think about their health needs and to promote a healthier lifestyle. The routines of residential life, choices about food, access to regular exercise and support with problems of alcohol, drug and substance abuse can all be used to support a young person in taking decisions to try to live differently. Again these are not just matters for health care professionals. Encouraging a young person to think about personal health issues or the kind of lifestyle that they want to pursue in the future and supporting a positive approach to these issues is something that a member of care staff or a prison officer can readily undertake. The area of sexual health and relationships is another very important one for young people. The different and specific needs of young women and young men need to be recognised and addressed in the design and delivery of programmes but also through the availability of relevant activities in the wider and more general regime.

The high levels of drug, alcohol and substance misuse amongst young people in custody are well documented. The time spent in a secure unit represents an ideal opportunity for a young person to receive both specialist help and general social reinforcement in their efforts to stop using substances. In the prison service significant resources have been invested in drugs workers and programmes for young people. Routine drugs testing and the development of 'drugs-free units' through the introduction of voluntary testing are particularly successful strategies for supporting young people in dealing with this problem. Similarly in local authority secure units and secure training centres resources are increasingly being linked into establishments to help young people with these problems.

Discussions about the mental health needs of young people in secure units usually focus on the issue of the insufficient numbers of forensic adolescent psychiatrists in post and the consequent difficulties in obtaining the necessary assessments, diagnoses and treatments that young people require. This is undoubtedly true and reflects a national problem which not only affects young people placed in secure accommodation but also young people in the community at large. There is an acknowledged national shortage of in-patient forensic beds for adolescents, and consequently many of the young people who would more appropriately be looked after in hospital are having to be kept in secure units with staff who are not trained or equipped to provide the proper nursing care that they need. As with other aspects of service provision to secure units there are widespread differences in the level of services provided from area to area and in the arrangements for how these services are organised and managed. Although the issues about the recruitment and training of consultants in forensic work with adolescents are not going to be solved in the immediate future, the Youth Justice Board have made the lack of mental health provision another of their immediate and main priorities and are working closely with the prison service and the National Health Service to remedy the situation and to put in place both interim remedies and a longer-term strategic plan.

In order for staff to be able to work positively and to develop an overall approach to a 'healthy' unit, definitions of mental health need to be more inclusive than just covering those young people who are seriously mentally ill, need to see a psychiatrist, and may require transfer to hospital. The way in which mental health services are organised in secure units obviously requires oversight by a senior psychiatrist. Diagnosing mental illness in adolescents is notoriously difficult and often complicated by such factors as a young person's drug and alcohol abuse. However, much of the day-to-day work can be undertaken by nursing staff working alongside prison officers or care staff whose training should include a basic introduction to the mental health needs of young people. Although there is no question of residential staff undertaking assessments or making diagnoses, we have already described how through their daily work with young people on a unit they can gather and collate important information about such things as mood swings, depression, general presentation and social behaviour. There is no doubt that the general atmosphere and climate on a unit contribute significantly to either promoting sound mental health and the general well-being of the young people who live there or exacerbating the problems that they may already have and even creating new ones. For some young people the mental health problems they experience pre-date their admission to secure accommodation and may have been part of the reason for their offending and subsequent placement in a secure unit. Placement in a secure unit may serve to emphasise or highlight these problems and immediate treatment will be required. For others the experience of being locked up may make them feel depressed or anxious to the extent that they too will need specific help. The creation of a positive culture on a unit in which staff pay attention to the needs of the young people in their care, get to know them, and in which everyone feels safe and secure goes a long way to alleviating lower levels of mental health problems and also provides a much better environment for the assessment and diagnosis of more serious problems.

In this chapter we have explored in some detail the range of work undertaken by staff and the importance of the roles that they play in shaping the overall experience of young people in secure units and in making that experience an opportunity for personal growth and development. All of these contribute to helping young people achieve the aim of not re-offending on release. We have also put this work into a wider context of the whole range of activities and services that make up the elements of the regime, and we have emphasised how the basis of this has to be the provision of a safe and secure environment for all who live and work in the secure unit. All of this needs managing and it is to this that we now turn.

Chapter 7

The art of management?

There is sometimes a debate about whether management is an art or a science. Many definitions of art include the idea that, at least in part, a work of art in any form should invite its audience to stand apart from daily routine and reflect on wider meanings. To create such opportunities for thinking within what is a busy and frenetic world, whilst at the same time looking after highly delinquent and severely damaged young people, must be considered an art indeed! It is essential, however, that space for thinking is made and that slots of time are worked into the pattern of the week so that managers and staff are able to reflect, think about their work and take stock of what is going on around them. Secure units are complex organisations doing difficult work, and looking after damaged and delinquent children or young people poses some very troubling questions for society which provoke very ambivalent responses about the role and purpose of such institutions. Secure units are also volatile organisations, subject to powerful external forces yet at the same time expected to contain equally powerful and highly charged emotional pressures generated from within. Almost more than any other kind of organisation these units are places of ambiguity and uncertainty. As Pascale and Athos put it:

> The inherent preferences of organisations are clarity, certainty and perfection. The inherent nature of human relationships involves ambiguity, uncertainty and imperfection. How one honours, balances and integrates the needs of both is the real trick of management.
>
> (Pascale and Athos 1981: 105)

This exemplifies the dilemma to the full, for it is precisely human relationships, in all their rich diversity and uncertainty, that create what we have previously described as the life-blood of secure units. We have already identified that predictable and reliable routines in a secure unit are major contributors to establishing and maintaining a safe, secure and containing environment which promotes the personal development and growth of young people. We have also recognised the ways in which relationships between staff and young people may impinge on the functioning of a secure unit and how this needs to be clearly understood by all those who work within it. This chapter is about how those processes are best managed, not only within the secure unit, but also externally by those who as line managers have specific responsibilities.

The need for effective management in secure units cannot be underestimated. A primary task of a secure unit is to manage and challenge the chaotic behaviour of the young people who are admitted. If the unit itself is chaotic in the way that it is organised or if staff are uncertain about their roles and tasks, then the chaos that is brought into the unit and manifested in the behaviour of the young people converges with the institutional chaos in ways that are likely to be explosive and destructive. As Hinshelwood puts it:

> Poorly organised institutions will risk enhancing the internal disorganisation of their severely disordered members, who in turn will tend to dismantle and disturb the organisation of the institution.
>
> (Hinshelwood 1999: 42)

The focus of this chapter is on the dynamic tasks of managing and leading staff groups rather than on developing models of management and leadership *per se*. In other words it is the work that managers do and the ways in which they provide leadership with which we are concerned. Within what is now defined as the juvenile secure estate there are different types of secure unit with separate management structures and organisational frameworks. Nevertheless, irrespective of these differences, common issues and problems emerge for managers which they have to resolve. As with groups of staff, when managers from different types of secure accommodation get together and are asked to identify their most pressing concerns, they do not take long to agree an agenda. Although our focus is on the specific issues that arise from managing secure units it should not be inferred that there is not much to be learned from a wider study of management theories or from drawing upon the experiences of successful senior managers in other kinds of organisations. However, the dynamics that arise from two significant factors – first, that it is a locked institution and, second, that it is young people who are locked up – are unique, and these dynamics have a direct impact on managers and on the processes which have to be managed.

Dealing with emotional realities

Traditional descriptions of organisations and how they operate tend to concentrate on such matters as their structure, aims, roles and tasks, or the systems and procedures which are designed to ensure that overall organisational goals are successfully achieved and the work of staff is regulated and monitored. 'Emotional realities' is a term that denotes a way of thinking about certain factors which may not be quite so easily defined as the areas above but consideration of which is nevertheless vital to gain a full appreciation of the real substance and purpose of an organisation. A great deal of emotional material is generated in secure units by those who work and live within them. It is a mistake for managers of these facilities or similar organisations to ignore the strength of these feelings or to disregard the powerful influence that they have on the way staff react and behave in the course of their work. It is not just that people get 'worked up' by what they do; the processes involved are much more complicated than that. Relationships that develop between adults and young people as they live alongside each other and share in the here and now activities of daily life inevitably arouse deep-rooted and painful memories which echo each young person's recent and more distant past. To this extent, surfacing emotions is an intrinsic part of the work that goes on inside a secure unit, but it is the content of these emotions that is also significant and which has implications for managers. As we have already shown, the most commonly expressed basic feelings of both staff and young people in secure units centre around the twin fears of isolation and of being attacked. It is important to recognise at this point that managers experience exactly the same feelings. In a seminar on management and leadership organised as part of the third University of Sheffield Conference on 'Working in Secure Units' which took place in December 2000, managers were asked to identify the most problematic aspects of their job and their main sources of stress. Almost without exception they identified a lack of training opportunities to prepare them for the challenges of a management role, and lack of ongoing support as they assumed the responsibilities of their new positions. Along with this absence of training were allied feelings of frustration at the way competing demands and unrealistic expectations were placed upon them by their line managers. They also felt very vulnerable to criticism about their performance which they anticipated could come from a variety of different sources.

In an account of their work as management consultants in one of the three Special Hospitals which look after the most dangerous of mentally disordered offenders in England, Hutton, Bazalgette and Armstrong identified the feeling of vulnerability as key to helping the hospital managers understand something about the emotional realities of their organisation. As this theme was identified by a very senior manager reflecting on his own experience in the organisation, the consultant put back to him the question, 'how far are you focusing on feelings which are more widespread throughout this organisation? Seen in that way, could your own experiences of isolation and vulnerability be understood as being part and parcel of being in touch with the life of the organisation?' (Hutton *et al.* 1994: 192). Realising that feelings of isolation and vulnerability permeate these types of organisation – that they are part of what has to be managed or that they may provide important clues about the real nature of the task and the needs of staff and clients – is an important step for all managers to take:

> Seen from this perspective, the managers' experience of feeling isolated and vulnerable could be understood as registering in themselves an emotional experience that was part and parcel of the life of the organisation as a whole; that arose out of and in turn illuminated the very nature of the task upon which all members of the organisation were engaged, staff and patients alike. As such these experiences were not so much an 'occupational hazard' as the raw material for work .... Correspondingly, the monitoring of these experiences and their fluctuations within oneself, could be seen as a central aspect of the practice of management and leadership, of keeping in touch and of being in touch.
>
> (ibid.: 193)

If managers, staff and young people in secure units are exposed to and share common feelings around their own and others' vulnerability, then this is also the case for people who live and work outside the walls. Any contact they may have with a secure unit inevitably evokes feelings about their own vulnerability, which may not be always welcome or readily acknowledged. We have already discussed the ambivalence which people have towards the role and functions of secure units and the ways in which this can affect those who work inside them. In order to manage a secure unit effectively, managers must not only be in touch with the emotional realities inside the secure unit but also in touch with and able to contain the extraordinarily high levels of anxiety that such institutions generate externally. There are a great number of people who are in some sort of relationship to secure units, either through their professional role, as members of the local community within which a secure unit is located, or as members of the general public concerned about how society as a whole treats delinquent young people. To put it another way, all of these groups are to a greater or lesser extent stakeholders in secure units and their views and perspectives have to be taken into account when defining the role and purpose of any particular secure unit. It must also be recognised that both the local and national media play an important part in determining views held about either an individual secure unit or the wider system as a whole. The model in Figure 7.1 illustrates the complexity of the relationships with which managers both inside secure units and externally have to engage.

A further dimension to the emotional realities within a secure unit arises from the adolescent and delinquent nature of the groups who are placed in them. Adults, irrespective of their age, are brought face to face and work in close proximity with adolescents whose experiences are likely to have been highly disturbing and whose behaviour is extremely delinquent. The feelings that are aroused through working in this intense environment may become overwhelming and frightening for staff. If such powerful emotions are either ignored or suppressed, and consequently not appropriately contained, they inevitably emerge through delinquent, disaffected or deviant forms of behaviour amongst the staff group. This takes many forms and may be observed through such occurrences as frequent and recurring lateness to staff meetings, unexplained absences from work, avoidance of supervision, important information not being relayed from shift to shift at handover meetings, or cancelling and missing key worker sessions. All of these may be tell-tale signs of high levels of stress, either within individuals or the whole staff group, and must be addressed by the management team.

What do managers do?

Having a clear understanding of the issues raised above, however, is not sufficient in itself. Managers have to do more than think, although that is a much underestimated skill and a very much neglected part of the traditional management role. Managers actually have to manage; that is, on a day-to-day basis, they are required to do such things as assess information and plan accordingly, allocate resources and make decisions. Mintzberg attempts to answer what at first seems a straightforward question: what do managers do? Finding an answer is a much more complicated matter:

> The manager must design the work of his organisation, monitor its internal and external environment, initiate change when desirable and renew stability when faced with a disturbance. The manager

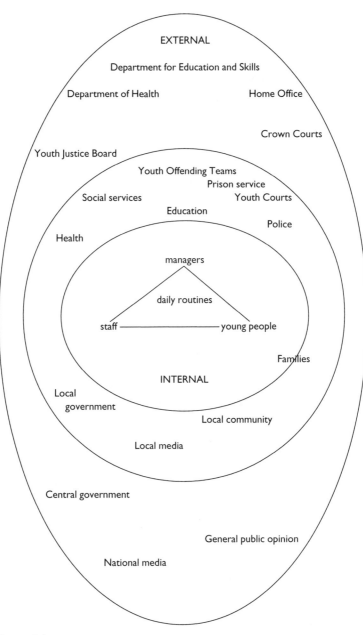

Figure 7.1

must lead his subordinates to work effectively for the organisation and he must provide them with special information some of which he gains through the network of contacts that he develops.

(Mintzberg 1973: 169)

A key part of a manager's role is to ensure that the necessary structures and systems are in place to support the work of staff and that the programmes for the young people are delivered. Not only do such structures and systems have to be in place but they have to be sustained, particularly when the organisation is under pressure. Even at the best of times there always seem to be more things to do than time or people to do them. Additional pressures such as staff absences, which run at notoriously high levels, only serve to make things more difficult. Having in place functioning systems which ensure the regular occurrence of team meetings, handover meetings, supervision and training, is essential in maintaining purposeful work from the staff group and in providing for them the necessary space for reflection and learning. Managers have to believe in these activities and be prepared to make tough decisions about their priority at times when other pressures come to bear. There are various problems for managers in these circumstances. The immediate demands of the young people never go away, and however many staff are off sick or away on leave these demands still have to be met. Achieving a balance between meeting the needs of staff and meeting the needs of young people requires not just good organisation but imagination and commitment. Establishing in the culture of a unit the expectation that staff have a right to their own space and time is difficult to achieve when the young people make their needs known in very direct and obvious ways and seem almost to be issuing a challenge: ignore me if you dare! Unless this is managed properly, a sharp, competitive edge may develop between the staff group and young people: 'This is our time' or 'We never get time for ourselves' are not unusual comments by staff in a busy secure unit, and at least acknowledging these pressures and being able to talk about them with staff and young people is a beginning.

One of the things that happens in a secure unit is that both staff and managers become infected with a sense of helplessness about situations. Staff blame managers for the fact that nothing seems to change, and managers blame their managers, right up to the point where the chain goes outside of the unit to 'them out there'. It is useful to be able to think that this sense of helplessness may reflect something of the powerlessness of young people locked up in secure units, but managers have to be able to do something about it as well.

Examples of having to deal with what are ongoing issues for all managers are unauthorised staff absences and lateness. These are two of the biggest bugbears for managers, and just holding hands up in the air and bemoaning the state of the world is at best defeatist and at worst a collusion with the sort of adolescent and delinquent attitudes which can become pervasive throughout the whole organisation. Failure by a management team to confront and deal with such matters sends out the message not only that staff cannot be contained but also, by implication, that nothing can be done for the young people in the unit either. The issue then is not just helplessness but hopelessness and that is much more profoundly damaging. Of course a high rate of staff absence might be linked to the fact that other needs are not being met and staff are not being supported and adequately contained through staff meetings or supervision. However, there are occasions, even when these are being provided, where the issue of absenteeism is a problem. In these circumstances managers have to do something and the best way is usually through straightforward management approaches. In one local authority secure unit the council's system for monitoring and recording absences is rigorously pursued and staff are followed up on their return to work and interviewed accordingly. In addition to this, through a system of small rewards and presentations, the unit has developed its own ways of acknowledging those staff who attend work regularly and don't take time off. Senior managers have to balance their understanding that secure units are tough places to work in with a realistic approach to tackling poor staff performance. Their responsibility is to ensure that mechanisms for staff support are in place, to monitor their effectiveness and to provide support to their middle and first line managers who may find it hard to confront staff over poor performance. Partly this is because of the nature of the organisation and the kind of work staff do, and partly because first line managers, at least, may still work on a shift pattern with the members of staff they manage, be closely involved in their day-to-day issues and also rely on them for support in difficult or dangerous situations.

We have identified that common feelings are shared by all managers in secure units and that these feelings are part and parcel of the nature of the organisation, the type of work that it does and the ambivalence in wider society about its role and purpose. Although there may be common elements to this emotional content amongst managers at all levels, the ways in which they approach the tasks of the organisation differ according to their roles.

External management

The juvenile secure estate is made up of three types of secure unit: Young Offender Institutions, secure training centres and local authority secure units. Each of these types of unit has a different external organisational framework.

Young Offender Institutions are part of the prison service and subject to the regulations and procedures of the service as a whole. Although over the years there have been different arrangements within the service for the management of different parts of the prison estate – e.g. high-security establishments, women's prisons and establishments for under-18-year-olds – there is still an overall structure of management within which these different types of establishments are placed. Line management accountability of the Governor, as the Senior Manager is called, in those Young Offender Institutions which admit only young people under the age of 18 years is to the Assistant Director of the Juvenile Operational Management Group. This person has sole line management responsibility for certain establishments and partial responsibility for those Young Offender Institutions in which both under- and over-18-year-olds are placed.

Secure training centres are owned by independent companies who provide contracted services to the Youth Justice Board. The centres are themselves part of larger companies, and their Directors, as the Senior Managers are called, are accountable to a manager who represents the wider business interests of the parent company.

Local authority secure units are each managed by a different local authority and situated within the management structure of their social services departments. The Senior Manager of a local authority secure unit is designated by a variety of titles: Principal, Centre Manager, Operations Manager or just plain Manager being the most popular. In this chapter we shall use the term Centre Manager as a generic term to cover all of the titles used in the local authority secure units, and the term Senior Manager when referring specifically to the Head of each type of secure unit. The person to whom the Centre Manager is accountable within the social services department varies from authority to authority and depends on the size of the secure unit, a factor which also determines their level of seniority within the social services hierarchy.

This diversity in external management arrangements clearly impacts on the way in which the Senior Managers in the different types of secure unit approach their work. However, although there are differences in the wider organisational structures within which Young Offender

Institutions, secure training centres and local authority secure units are set, from the point of view of all managers in secure units there are similarities in the pressures and problems they face. Governors, Directors and Centre Managers are all accountable to an external authority and are required to act as intermediaries between that authority and their own organisation. The key issues for all of them are that they have to manage a number of boundary issues with their wider organisation and apply a whole series of policies and procedures to their unit which may well have been designed for quite different purposes and for application in very different settings. These policies and procedures cover a number of important administrative areas including personnel, recruitment, selection and training of staff as well as financial and purchasing systems. They also include policies and procedures directly related to practice, such as child protection, complaints and casework. In the prison service and also in local authorities, many of these policies and procedures are widely used across different types of settings and have been devised with a general application in mind. The details of all this vary but the common element is that in every secure unit a range of policies and procedures have to be filtered into the unit and applied in a way that is relevant to the needs of staff and young people. This may be experienced as a constraint by managers and staff in secure units who feel that they are the ones best placed to understand the requirements of their unit and to develop appropriate policy and procedural responses.

The way in which a secure unit relates to its wider, external world is very much the responsibility of the Senior Manager. Their relationship to the external authority largely shapes the way in which other staff, both within and without the unit, view each other and the kind of working relationships that they establish. The relationship between the Senior Manager in a secure unit and their immediate line manager is critical and needs to be worked at in a serious way. For the relationship to work well there has to be a mutual respect for the different roles that each plays and a mature understanding of the different pressures with which each has to deal. Senior Managers in secure units have to feel that their line manager understands the operational demands of the establishment and is prepared and able to offer support, not just in times of difficulty and crisis but in making headway with those recurring mundane and knotty problems – for example, in the area of personnel. Line managers must have confidence in the competence of the Senior Manager in a secure unit and also be assured that the pressures that they face in their role outside of the unit are understood. For line managers these pressures are most likely to be in such areas as achieving financial targets or being held accountable for some other set of performance measures delivered from their own higher management. These relationships have to be open and allow for information to be freely exchanged, so that Senior Managers in secure units are given access to a wider perspective on their service or to developments within the wider organisation, and line managers are able to feel confident that they know what is going on in the unit and are not going to be caught out by some unwelcome news arriving on their desk in a report on the front page of a local paper.

Understanding respective roles, sharing responsibilities, supporting and enabling are the main ingredients of these relationships. What gets in the way? Professional rivalries and envy are not unknown, and unfortunately people are very prone to think that they can do someone else's job better than the person in post. Beneath some of the more obvious human failings, however, the real anxieties in these jobs have already been identified. The feelings of vulnerability and isolation experienced by a Senior Manager in a secure unit, which come from the very nature of the organisation and its tasks, can all too easily impinge on the way in which they see the world around them, and over time they can begin to experience it as threatening. External line managers carry enormous anxieties about the potential for disaster in the secure unit for which they are responsible, and are the recipients of many of the hostile projections and fantasies from people outside the unit, the content of which usually relates to some sort of violence or sexual perversion that they imagine must be going on inside the walls. Part of the responsibility of these managers is to hold on to and contain these anxieties in a way that allows other staff to be freed up to do their work. If the working relationship between the two managers can allow for these anxieties to be acknowledged and thought about, then there is a much stronger likelihood that the task of containing them will be successfully accomplished. The reality of external authority should neither be an overwhelming constraint that has to be resisted at every opportunity nor an excuse for inactivity and inertia on the part of Senior Managers.

In Chapter 3 we considered the beginnings of three units and the importance of containment for their successful development. All of those units involved complex relationships with their managing organisations and surrounding communities. In particular there was a very high level of interest and concern from local councillors and indeed the council as a whole. Inevitably there were strong differences of opinion between different councillors about the worthwhileness of the project and its possible impact on the local community and beyond. Whilst some were very supportive, others were more vocal in their opposition. Providing containment for what were very high levels of anxiety about the units was important not only for the adults and young people who were the first staff and residents, but also for those external to the units which included the local council officers and members. This became increasingly important as things went wrong and potentially high-profile incidents occurred. The role of the immediate line manager was crucial in helping to defuse the panic of crisis, but more importantly in taking a pro-active role by creating and using opportunities for defining the role and purpose of the unit, the nature of the work being undertaken and the risks involved. The question still arises, however, about who contains the anxiety of the external manager. In two cases they found support in the wider management of the organisations within which the units belonged. In the third this organisation was itself so dysfunctional at senior management levels that appropriate support could not be provided, and in the end this took its toll in the resignations of both the first internal and external managers.

An unavoidable and essential part of the job of a Senior Manager in a secure unit is, therefore, to work closely with their line manager in order to maintain a reasonable balance between external and internal pressures and to act as a buffer between the unit and the outside world. In practice this means creating systems so that policies and procedures devised externally can be appropriately filtered and become relevant to the unit's own functioning, and also providing a measure of protection from the negative and hostile projections which a secure unit inevitably attracts. A Senior Manager who has established a good working relationship with their line manager is more likely to achieve these aims than one who has not.

Managers as role models in the organisation

Despite the fact that a good deal of policy and procedure is prescribed for managers in secure units they nevertheless have an absolutely crucial role in determining how those policies and procedures are applied. More importantly, however, it is the actual behaviour of the Senior Manager, along with that of all other managers, which embodies the culture of the organisation and sets the tone as to what kind of unit it is. The importance of positive role modelling extends right through the organisation. It is one thing to have a vision statement and clearly stated values and expectations about the behaviour of staff; it is quite another to live these out in the busy and demanding day-to-day world of work. Closing the gap between rhetoric and practice is part of management responsibility in all areas of an organisation's functioning, and for this to be achieved requires a willingness to talk about issues and defining the space and time for this to occur. Attempts to explore this may be helped by using the idea of 'theory espoused and theory in use', which draws attention to the differences which may exist in organisations between the assumptions which are said to guide the actions of managers and the assumptions which actually do guide them.

At a morning handover in a secure unit a manager comes into the meeting and asks a question about how things were the night before. In that secure unit there is a management policy that staff on duty have fully delegated authority to make decisions and to act as they feel the situation demands. This is the theory espoused. However, staff know from experience that this is not really the case and that probably any action they do take will not be supported by their managers, and that they might well be liable to disciplinary action if things go wrong. In other words, if decisions need to be taken it is safer to pass them up through the line management structure, and so, in practice, all decision making is in fact delineated by position within the hierarchy rather than by the role taken on by a member of staff in a situation. This is the theory in use. Having clearly defined boundaries around decision making and being clear about who can decide what and when, and yet at the same time respecting the need for operational decisions to be taken across those boundaries, are not necessarily mutually exclusive positions to hold. What is required is that actual events and experiences are openly and regularly analysed in order that underlying assumptions can be exposed in examples from practice.

At another morning handover, staff coming on duty ask the staff group who were on shift the previous evening about the events of the night. The secure unit's stated expectations are that young people should be confronted about their antisocial behaviour and that any poor behaviour they might exhibit will be directly challenged. This is the theory espoused. In the handover the question is asked, 'was it a quiet night?' The assumption underlying the question is that a quiet night is a good night and what should be striven for is not to stir things up but to keep the lid on. This is the theory in use. It is very easy for managers to look for a quiet night, and staff quickly become aware of those managers who do not want to hear bad news and who are liable to shoot the messenger!

We have already seen that in order for information to flow freely a consistent structure of meetings is essential. It is the Senior Manager and other managers who determine the frequency of meetings across the establishment, define their purpose and stipulate who should attend. Given that at least in this respect it is managers who set the agenda for the organisation it is amazing how many meetings take place in secure units where the young people are not even acknowledged as a presence in the unit yet alone talked about in terms of their relevance to the purpose of the meeting.

Of course some meetings are about other things: drains, roofs, heating systems, building maintenance and so on are perfectly legitimate topics for certain meetings. It is also the case that for a good deal of the time logistical matters have to be discussed – e.g. rosters – because detailed planning to ensure the smooth running of such a complex organisation is essential. Of course not every meeting necessarily involves psycho-dynamic explorations of underlying cause and meaning. However, re-membering the staff meeting devoted to the topic of toothpaste, it must never be forgotten that the purpose of a secure unit is the care and treat-ment of delinquent young people, or that the dynamics set up by the inter-actions of these young people with the adult staff group may impact on every level of the organisation.

At a meeting of secure unit managers from across the country each manager was asked to provide a brief summary of recent developments in their unit and to highlight their main area of concern. A number of units had recently completed a major refurbishment of their facilities and at least two new units had recently opened. As the round-up went on each manager in turn talked about the problems they were experiencing with their building programme: roofs were leaking; electrical locking systems kept failing; heating systems were erratic; doors were not fixed properly. After some while a brave manager said something about how even after a good induction programme the staff were not really prepared for the difficulties presented by the young people in the unit and were having severe problems trying to settle them into the newly opened building. The silence that greeted this contribution was something akin to the social gaffe of breaking wind in church. It was quite clear that protocol demanded the avoidance of such issues and that it was not safe to try to address the fact that the real source of concern for these managers and their staff groups was not in the frailties of a building but in the contain-ment of the young people's anxieties expressed through very difficult behaviour.

Formal and informal sources of management information

The varying nature of the work in a secure unit means that no single approach to the management task is sufficient. The challenge for managers is to identify an appropriate style for each individual part of the organisation and to ensure that the right mixture is achieved so that the organisation as a whole runs smoothly and effectively. We have previously described the different staff groups and the range of services that they have to deliver to sustain the twenty-four-hour residential regime. Although all these tasks must be underpinned by a common set of values and principles to which everyone in the secure unit subscribes, different types of work require different arrangements for their administration and organisation. As Handy comments with reference to conformity and the way in which different kinds of cultures can co-exist within the same organisation:

> Differences, then, are necessary and good for organisational health. Monotheism, the pursuit of a single god, must be wrong for most organisations. But the choice and blend of gods cannot be haphazard. The wrong god in the wrong place means pain and inefficiency.
>
> (Handy 1978: 50)

To manage the residential task successfully requires an understanding of the formal and informal processes by which staff and young people negotiate the business of a secure unit and which arise from its dual function as a place in which young people live and adults work. The organisation of work entails systems, structures and formal administrative and financial procedures. There are statutory requirements for the proper documentation of various kinds of information and for formal records to be kept. These systems and procedures are subject to formal inspection or audit, and their design and maintenance mean that staff must take a systematic and consistent approach to their work.

Staff who are recruited to administrative or financial posts have different expectations about the work from those staff who are recruited to posts more directly concerned with the care of young people. On a day-to-day basis the priorities of administrative staff are different from those of their residential worker colleagues, but at a more fundamental level the environment may well arouse emotions in them with which they are unfamiliar. The experience of seeing and hearing about the young people during the course of their working day may be disturbing and cause them to be put in touch with previously unknown personal needs and feelings. Management support must be offered to all staff not directly involved in the care and management of young people, because experience shows that, if these feelings are not acknowledged and talked about, there are likely to be negative and serious consequences. Although there are variations in the ways in which these manifest themselves, depending on the area of staff's work, there are common themes which regularly emerge. These tend to focus around issues to do with the material care offered to young people and the perceived lack of control exercised by the residential staff over the behaviour of the young people. This gets expressed in such opinions as 'the young people in this unit are treated too well', or 'if only kids outside had the same opportunities', where comparisons are made between the 'lavish' resources available for activities within the unit and those of the impoverished world outside. The other commonly expressed view is: 'These kids in here do what they like and the staff have no control. If I was in charge ....' Of course, it is not just administrative or domestic staff who may have these feelings; they may be shared by care staff and prison officers as well from time to time. What tends to happen, however, is that the views become polarised between different staff groups, with the result that residential staff become very defensive and in turn are critical of the work done by the administrative, domestic, catering or maintenance staff. What this illustrates for managers is the way in which the central issues and concerns of secure units are the same at all levels. For society as a whole, for the wider organisation and in the secure unit itself, for both groups and individuals a balance must be preserved between meeting the obvious and demonstrable needs of the young people and fulfilling the role of the secure unit as a mechanism for social control. The task is to manage the boundaries between the levels so that in each area the issues can be dealt with appropriately. It is when the boundaries become permeable that chaos reigns. When a young person acts out the chaos of their internal world through their behaviour, staff must contain this and work with it to help the young person understand its meaning and develop alternatives. To achieve this, staff need strong and robust management support which is able to contain their anxiety through professional supervision and training, and which directs the work of the unit towards delivering the regime. Managers in a secure unit have to be supported by external managers who understand the internal dynamics of the unit and can share in the task of acting as a buffer between the unit and the ambivalence and anxiety which exist beyond its walls. If these boundaries do not exist and there is no containment, then the internal chaos of the young people, through the consequences of their acting-out behaviours, will extend beyond the unit and like wildfire wreak havoc in the already uncertain and ambivalent wider systems.

Secure units are organisations which generate different types of information and data, not all of which are of the sort that can be captured on a spreadsheet. The twenty-four-hour residential aspect of the task intro-

duces a unique dimension which is not found in conventional organisational life where most significant events take place in office hours and
where there is a clearer distinction between being or not being 'at work'.
It is within this dimension that the importance of what might be called informal organisational processes is located. Although all organisations
have this aspect within their culture, secure units more than most echo
with stories, myths and legends about characters from the past and
significant events that took place long ago but which still continue to
shape attitudes and beliefs about how things work and happen in the unit.
To gain a full picture of what a secure unit is like it is not enough to refer
to sheets of management information data, however useful they might be.
It is necessary to listen to the conversations that take place between
people and to listen to the stories that staff tell. These stories are like a
compendium of myths and legends which are an unofficial history of how
things have developed and why they exist as they do in the organisation.
Many of these stories revolve around comparisons with other organisations and how things are done elsewhere; they include the phrase 'that's
typical of us'; or, with a 'do you remember so and so', they refer to an
index of heroes, villains and fools who have played a part in the organisation's history. These characters may be staff who are still working in
the unit or who left years ago, but their exploits continue to be recounted
again and again. Young people, too, who made a significant impact during their time in the unit, also feature in these stories and have a part in
this unofficial history. Different staff groups, including managers, have
their own versions of the stories and ascribe the titles of hero, villain or
fool according to their perspective. Learning about what it is that these
people have done and why they are described in such terms reveals a
great deal about staff attitudes and opinions about the unit and their work.
Material of this kind is very powerful in institutions like secure units, and
this folklore about why certain practices continue is part of the reason
why it is so difficult to bring about change, particularly in older establishments. It is the case, however, that unless managers negotiate with
this material and take it into account, achieving any degree of organisational change or making even the slightest progress is likely to be significantly more difficult. The narratives that staff tell about a secure unit,
together with the stories that the young people bring, must be listened to,
processed and fed into the thinking that managers do to understand and
respond to the ever-changing circumstances around them.

It is a part of a manager's responsibility to bring these different and
sometimes conflicting approaches together and create an environment in
which there is mutual understanding and respect for the different types of

work that have to co-exist in an organisation such as a secure unit. A unifying factor is the recognition of the importance of structure within a secure unit, both in terms of its therapeutic significance for young people and in creating a stable organisational framework for the staff who are directly involved in their care. To this end all staff should be encouraged and required to ensure that any administrative tasks are completed as efficiently as possible. For care staff or prison officers, good recording and accurate writing about young people are an indispensable part of their work and a basic condition of sound professional practice. On the other hand administrative staff need to understand that their work is a means to an end and not an end in itself.

For a secure unit, 'hard' management information and accurate, relevant and current data, which assists managers in looking at key areas of the organisation's functioning and reveals trends across all areas of practice, are essential. Being able to identify recurring patterns in the time, place and circumstances of incidents yields information which can be used to provide helpful feedback to staff, which might, for example, enable managers to adjust the timings of certain regime activities in order to reduce opportunities for disruptive behaviour from young people. On the other hand, managers cannot afford to ignore the kind of information that emerges from the informal processes which are part and parcel of secure unit life. Being present and being around enough to engage with this kind of material through regular interactions with staff at all levels in the organisation is not a luxury for managers but an integral part of their work. Senior Managers in particular need to develop the capacity to acquire and balance these two kinds of information and to bring them together in a way that provides them and their middle managers with as full a picture as possible of the state of their unit.

Monitoring and inspection

As well as being able to relate effectively with external line management in their own, wider organisation, the Senior Manager of a secure unit has to engage with an ever-increasing number of bodies and individuals concerned with the monitoring and inspection of their unit. To be effective, all organisations must have in place mechanisms whereby their work can be monitored and their achievements measured. The Youth Justice Board has devised a collection of measures for the secure units against which a monitor checks the performance of the unit. The performance required is set out in a series of Service Level Agreements. Monitors attend the units on a regular basis, and the information they collect is collated and feedback is provided to units individually, and also collectively in the case of the prison service. This process is essentially concerned with the measurement of inputs, i.e. how much of the service is being delivered, along with outputs, i.e. how many times do certain activities occur. The system is not concerned with the quality of any of the activities it seeks to measure and as such is really only an extended way of ensuring that compliance with contract requirements is being achieved. In addition to this monitoring by the Youth Justice Board each sector of the juvenile secure estate has its own separate monitoring and auditing system. These systems reflect the wider concerns and priorities of a unit's managing body and are applied using a variety of methodologies.

Layered above these arrangements of auditing and monitoring are the national inspectorates which carry out regular inspections of each unit. In the case of local authority secure units there is in addition the local authority inspectorate service which currently inspects units for which the social services department has responsibility. The national inspectorates involved in the inspection of secure units are HM Prison Service Inspectorate, the Social Services Inspectorate and Ofsted, who inspect education provision across the secure estate. Under the auspices of the Youth Justice Board these inspectorates are beginning to come together and undertake joint inspections of secure units for young people. Inspection is a quite different process from audit and monitoring, being much more concerned with the quality of young people's experience whilst in custody and with the outcomes of their placement, i.e. what happens to young people in secure units. Inspection by the Department of Health's Social Services Inspectorate is against a laid-down set of national standards which cover areas of direct practice for the care and management of children and young people, as well as being concerned about aspects of security and the condition of buildings. Under the present arrangements it is quite possible for an individual establishment to receive a good inspection report and yet to be apparently failing in terms of audit requirements. As one very senior Governor put it, 'I'd settle for a good inspection report and a poor audit.' The implication that he was making is that a positive inspection report indicates a good establishment for young people and staff whilst the audit report tells more about administrative efficiency. Polarising these processes in quite this way, however, is not necessarily the best approach to achieving a method in which different kinds of data can be collated and used to inform the development of practice. As we have seen, relevant management information can be very directly used to influence decisions about the organisation of a regime, whilst in the same way audit information is useful for indicating aspects of a unit's performance, at least in terms of the level of input and output activity within the establishment. One of the main concerns at the present time is the emphasis that there appears to be on the monitoring and audit functions. This is further complicated by the multiplicity of audits and the different approaches that are taken as they are carried out. In the prison service this is complicated by the fact that the internal auditing systems are not as yet sensitive enough to the requirements of the regime for the age group being looked after and, although this is being addressed, there are still conflicts. The Youth Justice Board's monitoring system is currently a very blunt instrument and even though it will no doubt be amended in due course there remains the real danger that Senior Managers will become over-burdened with a plethora of audits, monitors and inspections.

The nature of the work undertaken by a secure unit demands that a more sophisticated approach be taken to evaluating its performance. The adage, it doesn't exist if you can't count it, is certainly inadequate in this context. The challenge for the Youth Justice Board and for the providers of secure accommodation has to be to develop a coherent and integrated approach to performance monitoring and inspection which can take into account the dynamic nature of the institutions and reflect the complexity of their task. This requires sophisticated systems so that a unit is monitored and inspected in a way which enables information to be collected about the level of efficiency in the delivery of regime activities and a detailed and informative narrative to be collated about the quality of the experience and outcomes for young people who are placed there. To bring these two aspects together assumes that a viable model is in place about what a secure unit for young people should be like, the level and kind of activities that should be delivered and the range of outcomes that are expected.

Tiers of management

In the following chapter we shall consider in detail the issues of career planning and progression for staff in secure units and in particular the training and development needs of managers. In this section we are focusing on the immediate issues that managers in a secure unit have to confront. In all the secure units that comprise the secure estate, managers operate at different levels and, although they may be called by various names in these different settings, each essentially performs the tasks which equate to the roles of first line and middle manager. There is a tier of managers who report directly to the Senior Manager in the unit and these too may be designated senior managers, but their roles are different. The distinctive role played by the designated Head of a secure unit – be that as Governor in a Young Offender Institution, Director in a secure training centre or Centre Manager in a local authority secure unit – is considered separately.

First line managers

Most first line managers in a secure unit work directly alongside their colleagues on shift rotations and take part in the day-to-day life and activities of the residential unit. Their daily responsibilities are usually focused on ensuring the smooth implementation of the unit's routines along with the delivery of the programmes for the young people. Invariably they are staff who have received promotion from the ranks of either care staff or prison officers, and generally they are selected for a management position on the basis of their aptitude in their original role. In most cases these posts are internal promotions. More than any other group in the wider management team these are the people who carry the model of practice for the unit and who are well versed in the needs of the staff and young people in the unit. These are the staff who know the formal and informal workings of the unit from the inside and have a wealth of experience about what is really going on. Making the transition from being a member of the team to having supervisory and management responsibilities is not easy and requires a good deal of support from senior colleagues. There are some obvious traps into which newly promoted staff may slip, not least being the dilemma as to into which 'camp' they fall when it comes to representing the needs of staff to their line managers and relaying management decisions back to their former staff colleagues. Although first line managers are likely to have a wide repertoire of professional skills and abilities to engage with young people, developing the confidence and the skills to pass these on to less experienced colleagues is another matter. These managers need specific training in supervision and coaching to acquire the teaching skills that their new duties demand. A similar set of skills is needed in taking on the difficult business of confronting colleagues with aspects of their performance which are not satisfactory. This may be really challenging if only a few months previously they were peer colleagues working together. To learn to be properly assertive in these situations and neither apologetic nor arrogant requires practice and feedback. This is a critical area in which managers at all levels need to gain competency, especially in the environment of a secure unit with young people. The capacity to be open and honest about the way another person is behaving, and to be able to explain the impact that this is having on other people, is a skill that is needed in order to relate effectively to the young people's group but also one that managers need to develop in their relationships with staff. The dangers of not doing this are serious for the integrity of the regime:

> Many managers in dealing with their subordinates eventually will take what seems to be the easier way out. Real feelings will be hidden, interactions will be of a ritualistic nature, platitudes will become the rule and lack of disclosure will lead to ambiguity.
>
> (Kets de Vries 1980: 56)

Middle and senior managers are making a wise investment of their time and energy when they put work into supporting and encouraging the development of their first line management group.

Middle managers

It is yet another leap to move from a first line management role to the responsibilities of a middle manager. These managers usually have responsibility for one or more living units in local authority secure units and secure training centres, or wings in a Young Offender Institution. They will generally be called Unit Managers in the former establishments and Principal Officers in the latter. At this level of management there is an increasing requirement to take a wider and more strategic view of the secure unit's functioning as a whole. Resource allocation and planning become more central to the range of duties undertaken and the time-frames within which these are required to operate are extended. Their line management responsibilities include a greater degree of delegated authority and their decision-making powers are increased. Unit Managers are more likely to become involved in other areas of work for the organisation and to share in establishment-wide cover duties. They may not have received any specific training for the additional and new duties which as middle managers they are expected to take on, and again they are likely to be internal promotions, having previously worked as first line management staff. However, in addition to the more defined management tasks that go with this role, middle managers are expected to have a good knowledge of the circumstances of the young people in their unit and also of the performance of individual members of staff. As first line managers are instrumental in the day-to-day delivery of the regime, so too are middle managers for ensuring the quality of the overall professional task in the secure unit. This group of managers experience in equal measure to their junior management colleagues the pressures of being in between. As their name implies, middle managers are an important bridge between their senior colleagues and the teams of staff working directly in the organisation with young people. For this group it is essential that they develop a sound working model of what the secure unit as a whole is about, and are given opportunities to reflect and think about how in their day-to-day work they are able to integrate their responsibilities for the professional practice of the unit with their more formal management tasks.

Senior managers

Between the middle managers and the Governor, Director or Centre Manager of each secure unit there is usually a tier of managers who may also be designated as senior managers and whose responsibilities generally include the delivery of a discrete area of service. This might be operations, education services, administration or facilities management. At this level within the organisation the primary tasks are much more about the overall resourcing of a particular area of service, longer-term planning, policy development and the monitoring of practice within their area of responsibility and across the establishment as a whole. Not only do managers at this level interface with staff from different disciplines across the establishment, but they also have important roles in dealing with external agencies. This includes a greater contact with, and awareness of, the wider organisational context in which their unit is set and the political dimensions within which this work takes place. As managers move further and further away from the details of day-to-day work in the organisation and their work becomes more strategic, with a longer-term focus and subject to the pressures of the external forces bearing upon the secure unit, so it becomes even more important that they are able to hold on to the core purpose for which the unit exists and the key principles which underpin its work. The extent to which this applies depends to a certain extent on the size of the secure unit. Irrespective of this, however, managers at this level in an organisation need to be able to accommodate the big picture in their thinking, but also to remember how small details and issues may affect the overall performance of the unit. This is a major contributory factor to what makes these jobs so difficult and partially, at least, explains why there are not queues of people waiting to take them up. At the higher levels of management in a secure unit, however large or small that unit may be, a constant tension is experienced between issues arising from the day-to-day dynamics of the exchanges between staff and young people and the wider demands on the unit from a host of external agencies.

Managing boundaries

Managing boundaries is a crucial aspect of the management task for all managers in a secure unit. These include the boundaries between different levels of management, between different disciplines and staff groups and between the unit and external agencies. For managers, knowing the boundaries to their role and being confident about the level of decision making they have within them is very important. The constantly changing and dynamic nature of a secure unit coupled with the speed at which incidents occur makes it very difficult to prescribe staff reactions and responses to cover every situation. This is not to say that there should not be clearly laid-down procedures to guide staff actions in certain circumstances. In fact there must be clearly established procedures to cover staff responses in the very predictable situations which occur. Prescribed responses to incidents relating to matters of safety and security in the establishment or child protection allegations are amongst the most obvious. Often, however, it is smaller matters which lead to the greatest frustration if managers are not sure what they can or cannot do. Even if a blueprint covering all eventualities cannot be handed down, it is possible to develop a working climate in which everyone, irrespective of their place in the management hierarchy, is held accountable for actions they take and given time and opportunity to talk about why they made a certain decision. Secure units need well-established procedures within which staff operate, but they also need a climate in which exceptions to rules must be explained and, if need be, challenged. If this climate is not created then first line and middle managers very easily become undermined by actions of senior colleagues who may not have all the facts at their disposal. This is particularly so in regard to decisions made about the management of young people whose capacity for splitting staff groups we have already seen. A young person who believes they can manipulate a senior manager to the detriment of staff with whom they are in close daily contact has a powerful and dangerous weapon at their disposal. There is nothing more frustrating for staff than for a senior manager to come on to a unit and begin to negotiate with a young person about an issue that to their mind has already been resolved. However, senior managers do have responsibilities to monitor the actions of staff and other managers and to ensure the fairness of their actions *vis-à-vis* young people. This can lead to conflict between staff and the management team, with first line and middle managers caught in the crossfire. This is why the prison service adjudication system has much to commend it, at least in principle, as it delineates a separate forum for conflicts to be assessed and dealt with. The problem with this system, however, is that it removes conflict resolution from the setting in which the conflict originally occurred, and it is too formal a procedure for dealing with a younger population. Increasingly there are some good examples of disciplinary systems being developed that are more sensitive to young people and in which staff can have some confidence as well. Where these have been developed they have emphasised principles of restorative justice and have been aimed at encouraging young people to reflect on their behaviour and seek to make amends in practical ways. Boundaries do not exist solely to define actions that can only be done outside them but also to define what actions are expected to be done inside them. In other words, managers have to be prepared to take up the proper authority that is delegated to them within their role. Avoiding action and constantly seeking to push decisions up the line is a symptom of various conditions from which an organisation may be suffering. Staff may feel genuinely afraid of what might happen if they make a poor decision. On the other hand they might feel afraid to make any decision, particularly if it is likely to be unpopular with colleagues or young people. Staff and managers come under all sorts of pressures, most of which are directly linked to the particular characteristics of the young people in their care. Helplessness and hopelessness are powerful examples of this and both breed a sense of unhealthy dependence which affects both young people and staff alike. The young people look to the staff group to meet their needs, the staff group look to their immediate managers to meet theirs, and those managers look above them in the same way. This paralysing sense of helplessness is fuelled if organisational structures are so rigid that every action has to be checked out and if in reality there is no properly delegated authority, only a centralised and all-powerful one.

The Senior Manager

Many of the above issues come together and are brought into focus by a consideration of the functions of the Head of a secure unit or, as the post may be designated, the Senior Manager. This person has a uniquely important role in setting the tone and style of the organisation and, through their expressed attitude and behaviour, in determining to what extent stated values are made real through day-to-day activities. It is likely to be the Senior Manager who has responsibility for co-ordinating the work of the discrete departments within an establishment, for negotiating the contracts with external agencies if this is the way in which services are provided into the unit, and for ensuring that the processes whereby staff meet and talk together are in place. The role demands both an inward- and an outward-looking perspective to be taken on almost all issues. The Senior Manager is responsible for maintaining the boundary around the unit and for managing the ways in which external agencies or authorities relate to staff and carry out their functions when these take place within the unit. One of the most challenging aspects in this area is the way in which the Senior Manager handles external agencies when they become involved in sensitive investigations that arise out of incidents or allegations, and especially where these concern child protection issues. The perspective of those who work inside children's residential units and secure units for young people on occasions seems to be that there is a body of opinion outside the residential setting which regards the very nature of residential care as abusive and that therefore any investigation into an alleged incident begins with the presupposition that abuse must have taken place. Not all of this feeling is paranoia; in some cases they really are out to get you! Professionals in residential care of all descriptions have generally never been very good at explaining their work and have often been made to feel like poor relations in professional discussions and arguments. They have also been guilty from time to time of imagining that no one outside their rather closed world really knows anything about young people, understands anything about residential work or realises how difficult it is. We have already tried to explore some of the underlying reasons for these feelings and why they impinge on work with young people and on the relationships between professionals involved in their care and management. Senior Managers have to be pro-active in developing relationships with external agencies and in establishing a place for their unit as part of the wider network of agencies in the local area. Local authority secure units have more of a track record in this regard than does the prison service, as it is only since the Youth Justice Board and a discrete estate for under-18-year-olds have been formed that prison service establishments have worked in liaison with social services departments and in particular with child protection agencies. Being comfortable with the workings of a local Area Child Protection Committee and understanding the statutory role of child protection teams is a new experience for most Governors. In their case, and for their staff as well, there have been some steep learning curves to be negotiated. It is right that all secure facilities looking after children and young people are subject to external scrutiny and that any concerns are properly investigated by independent agencies in co-operation with the secure unit. Of course it is also essential that the unit itself has properly devised procedures which have been developed in consultation with local protocols and that there is clear evidence that all staff in the secure unit have been briefed about these procedures and are aware of good practice in child protection. However, if a situation arises then the role of the Senior Manager of the unit is critical both in briefing the external agency and also in supporting and guiding their own staff teams. If properly constituted agencies have a role to play in the investigation of sensitive internal incidents then that role has to be respected and its work made as effective as possible. It is at this point and in these times that the Senior Manager requires the support of their line manager in identifying underlying anxieties and fears arising from the pervasive feelings of vulnerability they may be experiencing. In the same way the Senior Manager has to be able to contain those feelings for the rest of the staff team in order to allow them to work collaboratively with colleagues from outside the institution. A real difficulty in these situations is the way in which the responses and emotions of young people change very quickly and alter the mood of a secure unit in a very short period of time. Often secure units and external agencies appear to be working to very different time-frames. The processes of an investigation may extend over lengths of time which for young people and staff in a secure unit seem like an eternity, and the events that occasion an investigation are soon overtaken by a myriad of other matters.

There is another set of issues which also tests out the resolve and tenacity of the Senior Manager to maintain the values and principles of the unit, and that is when there is a breach of security in the establishment. These are the events that create huge anxieties in the external management chain and can lead to serious repercussions. The prison service knows to its cost what happens if prisoners escape. Not only may public confidence be destroyed but the political fall-out usually brings a draconian response, with security procedures increased and a prolonged cancellation of regime activities. Being able to deal with these issues in a way that is open and fair, without embarking on witch hunts, is only possible if this is the general, underlying approach taken by managers following any sort of serious incident. Part of the management task is to monitor on a regular basis all unit systems, including those that cover security, and to ensure that staff are thorough in all aspects of their routine work. These responsibilities are not optional. They are part of the 'slog' of the work which involves doing the mundane and ordinary things which go on day after day but are essential for the safety and security of a unit. Keeping staff fresh in their performance of routine duties is not easy, but it is vital, as these basic routines and duties are the foundations for all other work which may go on in the unit with the young people and without which everything else will fall by the wayside. Qualities absolutely required by the Senior Manager are the will and resolve to manage their unit and to keep on pursuing the core activities in such a way that they remain high on staff's agendas and at the front of their minds.

In Chapter 2 we explored a tradition of therapeutic residential child care, a significant feature of which is the historical importance of the role of the leader in the ongoing life of a therapeutic community. Many of these communities were built on the inspiration and charismatic leadership provided by their founders. In this model of leadership it is the personal qualities and strengths of the leader that become the cornerstone of the residential community and the reference point for almost all activity within it. The positive aspect of this model is that it provides for staff and young people a focal point of inspiration against which they may struggle but upon which they can utterly rely. The weakness of this style is that it creates a dependency, which of course has its purpose and therapeutic significance, but it can equally prevent staff from taking personal responsibility and limit opportunities for personal growth. Most seriously of all, this style of leadership is virtually impossible to replicate when the founder moves on and has to be replaced by another figure who may not be able to match the character of the previous post-holder. In many other respects as well leadership as defined in these terms is no longer viable, not just because of the inherent weaknesses in the model, but because of the sheer practicality of the ways in which services are now arranged and staff expect to organise their work and social lives. Even if the time for charismatic leadership of this description is passed there is no doubt that the responsibilities that come with taking on the Senior Manager role in a secure unit require more than just good management skills, essential though these are. An organisation like a secure unit requires a focal point for leadership and for authority which resides for better or worse in the Senior Manager figure who heads up the organisation. Young people and staff instinctively look for a leader and a single point of authority against which they can check their actions and from which they expect to receive feedback. To avoid this role under the guise of encouraging democratic and participative management principles is to miss an important point about the essential role of the leader as the ultimate container and about the nature of secure units. Although many of the threads which run through the organisation connect to the person at the top, the Senior Manager has to have the maturity to allow senior, middle and first line managers, along with residential and other staff, to have genuine space and authority to do their work. There are two things to be achieved here: on the one hand the institution needs a clear sense of direction and confidence in its leader to whom it inevitably looks for authority; whilst on the other hand all staff need to know that they too have responsibilities and that they are expected to function as competent adults and professionals. For the Senior Manager this involves taking risks in the knowledge that at the same time they are ultimately accountable for everything that goes on. Not to take these risks only serves to foster that unhealthy state of dependency into which both staff and young people are all too ready to fall. As staff have to be encouraged to take responsibility, albeit with support, so too do young people. It may be a struggle and many young people may be too damaged or vulnerable to accept fully the need for growth and change, but working towards this is a part of the basic purpose for which the unit exists and the responsibility cannot be avoided.

The responsibility of being the Senior Manager brings a specific set of pressures which have to be managed and for which training and ongoing support are essential. There is a real difference between being one of a team, even of senior managers, and being the Senior Manager. Feelings of isolation and accompanying vulnerability which we have identified as being so powerfully present in secure units are experienced most strongly and personally by the Senior Manager. We have previously considered the ways in which the processes of projection and transference impact on relationships within a secure unit. It is the Senior Manager who inevitably becomes the figure upon whom staff and young people focus their anxieties and fears or in whom they invest their hopes as being the person who can make things change for the better. The Senior Manager is a centre of attention and incessantly talked about in the organisation, often in relation to both their public and private life, with a good deal of speculation and rumour attached. The interest of the young people is often expressed through questions about personal relationships outside of the establishment, the size and nature of the car that the Senior Manager drives or how much money they earn. The interest of the staff usually turns to private affairs or to things supposedly said or done at work.

As the first Principal of a newly built secure unit I was heavily involved in the programme of induction training for the large groups of new staff coming to work in the establishment. As might be expected, the anxieties about what the work was going to be like, what was going to happen and would it all go horribly wrong were going sky-high as the time of opening drew closer. Throughout the induction training the issue of how staff could be allowed sufficient autonomy to do their work and to take responsibility for it whilst at the same time providing a containing and secure framework which offered direction and some rules to follow was one with which I and other managers constantly wrestled. The staff group oscillated between dependence, desperately wanting to be told what to do or how to do it, and fierce independence, accusing managers of interference and being overbearing. As part of all this a story began to circulate around the unit that I had taken the other managers into a room and had been heard shouting at them. What I had been allegedly shouting about was not the point; it was more that I was at last laying down the law and letting these managers know what I thought about them! The reality was that it never happened. The most interesting thing was that staff thought it might or could happen, and we were all able to talk about this in a large staff meeting which gave us another opportunity to reflect about the meaning of dependence and what kind of leadership was most appropriate in the situation we all faced.

Making the transition from being a senior manager to being the Senior Manager is a big leap and requires special training and ongoing support. The fact that this is not available is worrying and has resulted in a number of casualties in Senior Manager appointments that might have been avoided.

Stillness in chaos

If it really is part of art to achieve opportunities for reflection or some kind of stillness in the midst of chaos then good management has to be art because, as we have seen, for staff to begin to do their work they must have opportunities to think in the midst of the kind of chaos that is characteristic of a secure unit. Managing a secure unit brings with it the unenviable task of having to solve a never-ending stream of conundrums and resolving seemingly impossible problems. The question is posed time and time again: what do you do when there is nothing you can do? The next chapter picks up this theme of the impossible task and the issue of what sort of training staff really need to work effectively in a secure environment with young people.

Chapter 8

Making the impossible even more difficult

There can only ever be one answer to the question, what is the most valuable asset in a secure unit? It is the staff. Of course attention must be paid to the standard of the residential accommodation, the availability of resources for education and training, access to relevant materials to provide challenging offending behaviour programmes and facilities for physical and other kinds of leisure activities. However, to make the full use of these, in a purposeful way and for the benefit of young people, requires the presence on a regular and consistent basis of highly motivated and multi-skilled groups of competent staff who are committed to delivering the regime. In order to achieve this a team of managers must also be in place who share a clear vision of how they want the secure unit to be, and who collectively have the experience and skills to provide the organisational structures and leadership which sustain the day-to-day work. We have already seen how secure units are made up of multi-disciplinary staff groups working together. Teachers, psychologists, psychiatrists, probation officers, social workers and other professional groups are appointed on the basis of their own profession's arrangements for qualifying and post-qualifying training. Although none of the initial training for these professions necessarily prepares people for work in secure accommodation with adolescents, it may be reasonably expected that in their qualifying training they are equipped to develop the professional expertise which, given time and further experience, may be applied within this particular setting. This is not at all the case for those who make up by far the greatest number of staff in a secure unit, namely residential care staff and prison officers. Their work brings them into constant and direct contact with young people in what are probably the most critical tasks of all those performed in the residential unit. Given what we have previously described about the nature of this work and the demands made on staff, it would not be unreasonable to make the assumption that any person wishing to work in a secure unit with young people should have a proper professional training before so doing. It is not a great leap from that assumption to believe that such opportunities for formal initial training are therefore available and accessible on a regular basis. The astonishing fact is, however, that despite the importance of this area of social policy, for those staff who in so many respects carry the weight of responsibility for the experience of young people in custody, specific professional and qualifying training is not available. The work is difficult enough, indeed at times it seems as if the demands it makes border on the impossible, so that not having a framework of training and professional development for staff does indeed seem like making the impossible even more difficult!

The Youth Justice Board has set in place a number of strategies aimed at bringing together the different types of secure unit into a more co-ordinated and integrated juvenile secure estate working to common standards and forming part of a coherent youth justice system. Included within these strategies is the development of a comprehensive training and development programme for all staff employed in the youth justice system, with specific modules for staff who work in secure accommodation. We shall return to this later as clearly in aspiration it is a right-minded idea to establish a common framework of values and identifiable skills for staff working with young people in youth justice agencies and especially in secure units. A major challenge in trying to work towards a common model of training is that the current providers of secure accommodation draw upon different traditions of training and have different expectations about what training should be provided for staff and how this is best delivered.

The background to training provision

The recruitment of prison officers has been undertaken using two main approaches. Prison officers have either been recruited centrally on behalf of the prison service as a whole, or alternatively local recruitment has been the preferred method. The advantage of the latter is that it allows individual establishments to be more targeted in their specifications for staff and to base these on the role that the establishment plays in the prison service estate. The problem still remains, however, that recruitment is to the service as a whole and not solely to any one part of it. This includes those facilities which look after young people under 18 years. The effect of this on recruitment and initial training is that staff must be prepared for work in the whole range of prison service establishments, of which the under-18 estate is only a very small part. At the present time, although there are numbers of staff who have elected to work with this younger population, there are many staff whose initial recruitment was to work in adult male prisons, which is by far the largest sector. For a number of these staff involvement with under-18s represents a new and in some cases unwelcome career development. Within these parameters initial training, which is of approximately three months' duration, has focused on teaching aspects of what is known as 'gaol craft' and has combined periods of residential training with experience in an establishment. Partly as a result of time constraints this type of initial training has been able to make little differentiation between the varieties of work undertaken within the different types of prison service establishments.

Even with its obvious limitations prison service initial training has at least provided officers with a structured introduction to the work of the prison service and prepared them as far as possible for the kind of situations and scenarios that they might be expected to meet in the generality of their work. The same cannot be said for those whose introduction to work with young people in secure accommodation begins in a local authority secure unit. The history of training for staff in residential child care settings is essentially a saga of good intentions which are never quite matched by either the provision of the necessary resources or the sustained effort which would make them realities for the majority of the workforce at any one time.

Fundamental to all the discussions about what training is required for residential workers, and this has been consistently so at whatever stage the debate has been held, is an uncertainty and ambivalence about the value and status of the work. As we saw in Chapter 2, the pendulum of public opinion as to what is best for troublesome children swings over time between ideas about welfare and punishment. So it is with the wider issues of how to provide help for needy, but not necessarily delinquent, children. Different periods of history have reflected changing perspectives as to what is right for the welfare of children and consequently in their best interests. Despite at times being the main way in which children in need of care have been accommodated, residential work has never achieved the same status as other areas of social care. One of the reasons for this is that residential work has been equated historically with domestic and family duties, which themselves are poorly remunerated and laden with the implicit assumption that parenting and the care of dependent relatives are largely unskilled and undemanding responsibilities. Such beliefs go way back, as illustrated in the following description of the work of residential staff written in 1898 by a student employed by what is now NCH Action for Children. It makes for interesting reading:

> The children's home is a place where no gift comes amiss, where many and varied gifts are absolutely essential. You must be able to sew and knit and darn, to make and mend and mark. To see when a house or child is clean, and to show unwilling boys and girls how to produce cleanliness in house and person. To cook a little, to nurse a little, to trim dresses and make hats. To warn them that are unruly, comfort the feeble-minded, support the weak, be patient towards all men. To answer the children's questions, to read aloud to them, to tell them stories, to pray with them and for them. To improve their manners and their morals, their grammar and their tempers. To enter into their play and foster their ideals.
>
> (Bradfield 1913)

The result of all this has been that the basic workforce in residential services has never been regarded as on a par with other professions as these have emerged and acquired recognition over the years. This is particularly true in its relation to the social work profession, with which residential work has been most closely allied and of which it has often been regarded as a branch.

Over the past sixty years there has been a plethora of committee and inquiry reports occasioned either by some particular scandal in a residential setting or in response to concerns raised by individuals or pressure groups. Whatever their specific origin all of these reports have commented critically about the state of services for children in residential care settings, made recommendations for improvements and included references to the importance of staff training. The Curtis Report was a result of a call to inquire into the immediate post-war conditions of children living in residential care, and recommended that:

> training for a professional qualification, under the aegis of a Central Training Council in Child Care, be set up to include linked practical and theoretical training on household management, care of health and prevention of disease, child development, playing with children, basic lectures on social conditions and social services, the general study of culture (for the student's own benefit), record and accounts keeping and religious education, if desired.
>
> (Curtis Report 1946)

This report set in motion a number of developments and in 1947 the newly formed Training Council established courses of fourteen months' duration for care staff in children's homes.

Over the following twenty years these training programmes expanded and came to include staff from Approved Schools and mainstream boarding schools. However, despite this growth in training opportunities, the vast majority of residential staff still remained unqualified and untrained, with the sheer logistical difficulties arising from the numbers involved being a significant problem. At the same time as these developments were taking place the debate continued about the relationship between training for residential work and qualifications in generic social work. Following the development in 1971 of the Central Council for Education and Training in Social Work (CCETSW) it was accepted that training for residential work should be of the same length and standard as for field social work and that initial training should lead to a common qualification. The consequence of this over a period of time was the demise of the specialist training courses in residential work established post-Curtis and the development of the Certificate of Qualification in Social Work (CQSW). The curriculum of social work training as it has evolved over the last twenty years has never fully acknowledged residential work as a discrete area of professional practice requiring specific training, and the tortuous logistical problems of how residential workers are enabled to gain access to full-time training courses have remained the same. The introduction of the Certificate in Social Services (CSS) was yet another attempt to provide a more flexible qualifying route into social work, and was intended to appeal to residential workers as a more viable way to train and become qualified. However, this initiative did not achieve that objective and despite best efforts it remained a 'poorer sister' qualification to the CQSW. The current situation is that a single social work qualification, the Diploma in Social Work, continues to apply to both field social work and residential settings and that all the problems to do with the provision of specific and relevant training for residential workers remain unsolved.

Another constant and dispiriting feature of the model of full-time social work training as it has developed over the years has been the steady stream of staff who, on completion of their qualifying training course and despite having previously worked in children's residential services, take up a post in field social work. In 1985 figures from CCETSW indicated that on completion of a qualifying course some 76 per cent of students went into field work positions, with only 15 per cent entering residential work. In trying to find reasons for this Ainsworth had previously identified a range of issues:

> There is no clear analysis of the underlying reasons for the resistance of CQSW holders to seek positions as residential practitioners .... A probability, however, is that a combination of factors which includes such items as remuneration, living-in requirements and the resultant diminished control over personal life space, the curriculum content of qualifying programmes and long term career prospects all deter qualified social workers from entering this sector of social work service.
>
> (Ainsworth 1978)

In addition to the above it is relevant to note that the experience of staff returning to work in residential units following a period of training has not always been a positive one from the point of view of how they are received back into the organisation and how their skills and knowledge are put to use.

> Criticism is put forward by many residential staff about the limitations put on their role by insensitive and centralist management styles used in many establishments .... In many cases even when 'training' receives a notional high value in the stated aims of an organisation there exists a strange mis-match between the proclaimed intentions and actual behaviour of managers in relation to allowing staff to use and practise newly acquired skills. Conformity and compliance, so often the required characteristics of clients, are equally sought after in members of staff.
>
> (J. Rose and Staniscia 1989)

In spite of the difficulties, there have been a number of interesting and worthwhile initiatives to provide relevant and accessible training for residential workers, using distance learning, as in the Open University or the Gatsby Project, at a post-qualifying level such as the course in Therapeutic Child Care developed at Reading University, or in central government programmes such as the Residential Child Care Initiative. Particular mention should also be made of the work undertaken by the National Children's Bureau in the development of excellent induction material for staff beginning work in local authority secure units. This is a comprehensive package for the training of new staff which is very user-friendly and accessible for managers and less experienced supervisors.

More recently the emphasis in the field of social care with regard to the training needs of the workforce has been on applying the model of National Vocational Qualifications (NVQs) already used in a number of industries. These are based on the development and assessment of skills used in the workplace underpinned by a defined knowledge base which is deemed relevant to the task. These qualifications can be achieved at different levels, making them accessible to the whole workforce irrespective of role or position within an organisation. In many respects this model appears to offer a more productive approach to the training needs of residential workers, although there are still associated problems of resources for sustaining the level of assessment required and in streamlining the volume of paper work that is generated.

Initial training

The focus of initial qualifying training for those working in children's residential services has over the years become increasingly linked to mainstream social work training. For many people in residential posts, gaining access to a qualifying programme is still seen as a route out of residential work, which adds even more pressure to the attempt to increase the numbers of qualified staff working in residential care. Social work training is currently a two-year full-time programme, although there are a few opportunities for this to be undertaken on a part-time basis over a longer period. From 2003 full-time training will increase to a three-year period. The content of many of these Diploma courses makes only limited reference to residential work, and in addition the particular issues involved in working in conditions of security with children and young people are rarely addressed. Funding for places on these courses is difficult to arrange, and for most employers in both the local authority and voluntary sectors the number of staff to whom they are prepared to offer secondment on a full-time funded basis has reduced to a bare minimum. In any case the numbers of secondment places now available are at levels that make no difference to the overall status of the workforce. In residential work the huge logistical problem remains as to how a largely unqualified workforce can be given access to training opportunities for the length of time required for the qualifying courses. Clearly the NVQ model is a way of addressing this problem as it moves away from course-based training to formal accreditation acquired through the processes of ongoing learning in the place of work. The logistical problems, however, are still unsolved and, as we shall discuss later, there are questions about the sufficiency of this approach for the task involved.

If retention of staff in residential care post-qualifying is still a problem then it is inevitable that the recruitment of qualified personnel to lower-grade posts is almost impossible to achieve. In most local authority secure units and secure training centres recruitment at this level is about identifying people who may have potential for the work, who display positive values and who have a willingness and some demonstrable aptitude for learning. The previous work experience of staff recruited to these posts is widely diverse, ranging from some associated work with young people, perhaps in a voluntary capacity, to no associated experience at all. Even if sufficient numbers of staff can be attracted to advertised posts there is a subsequent heavy burden placed on in-house induction, supervision and training programmes, and these may not have any recognised accreditation attached to them.

The initial training received by people currently beginning work in the juvenile secure estate depends, therefore, on in which sector they take up employment, i.e. the prison service, local authority secure units or a secure training centre. The prison service has completed a significant overhaul of its initial training programmes, moving away from an almost entirely residential and college-based approach to a model that shares experiences between residential and establishment-based training where the purpose is to consolidate learning acquired at the prison service college. The content of this initial training has also broadened to become more experiential, with specific inputs made which are relevant to the area of service in which the new recruits will be working. This has allowed for some introductory training to be given around the particular needs of young people and the way in which the youth justice system impacts on prison service staff. The shift within the prison service to a separate and discrete area of provision for the under-18 population has not yet been accompanied by any real strategic development of a training programme for staff working with this group of young people. The generic training requirements for staff in prison service establishments still apply, and governors are faced with difficult choices about what training to provide for their staff teams trying to come to grips with the demands of this group of young people. The Youth Justice Board, in trying to establish the concept of a secure estate and to introduce the raft of new measures which have accompanied the Crime and Disorder Act 1998, have made it a mandatory requirement for all secure unit staff to attend a six-day course, 'Working Together', which attempts to provide a framework for multi-agency working by including the attendance of Youth Offending Team workers on the programme. This has met with mixed reactions with regard to both the content of the course and the logistical nightmare involved in making it happen on the necessary scale. A disappointing feature for the prison service has been the failure to comprehensively deliver the training programme, 'Working With Young

People in Custody', developed by the Trust for the Study of Adolescence. This programme, which has been extensively revised and extended, was originally developed specifically for prison officers working with young people aged 15 to 21 years in prison service custody. It is a modular programme which has as its foundation an experiential approach aimed at getting prison officers to recall aspects of their own experience of growing up and to relate these to the young people in their charge and the needs of an adolescent group being looked after in secure accommodation. Based on sound principles of child and adolescent development the modules introduce staff to the world of young people and help them to understand their needs. Recently developed modules also consider the mental health needs of young people in custody and the importance of creating a positive culture and environment in the residential setting. This training programme has the advantage of being able to be delivered by in-house trained staff on a rolling basis. It is much to be hoped that this programme will be recognised as compatible with further training introduced by the Youth Justice Board, as certainly for prison service staff it is an excellent introduction to working with young people in custody. For the prison service the question still has to be answered, to what extent the provision for young people under 18 years is a separate and discrete area of the service to which staff are specifically recruited and for which focused training is provided. Recruitment to working specifically with young people need not be a barrier to career development across the prison service but it has to be acknowledged that working with adolescents is a professional task in its own right and has very specific training requirements.

Even if training opportunities for staff working with young people are underdeveloped, prison establishments, as part of a national service, do at least have access to an extensive and well-resourced training programme for their staff. This allows a co-ordinated approach to individual career development and planning for the service as a whole. Staff wishing to progress along the route to senior positions know what pathways they need to pursue and what training they need to undertake. Although there is a continuing need for review and revision in the light of changing needs and demands on the service, there is an overall structure and strategy for training in place. The same does not exist for staff working in local authority secure units. The differences between the local authorities who manage the units are reflected in the level of resources they put into the training of staff working in the secure unit, and whether or not these resources are regarded as discrete or expected to be provided from out of the general training budget allocated to children's services within the social services department. It is certainly the case with induction and initial training programmes for staff recruited to a secure unit that for the most part whatever is provided has to be developed internally and subject to the resources available within the unit.

Secure training centres, a relatively recent addition to the range of providers of secure accommodation for young people, have developed their own training strategies in response to contract requirements and stipulations by the Youth Justice Board. As with other providers, these units have had to develop their own training strategy and devise their own curriculum using in-house personnel or consultants bought in to deliver the programme. Their specific role and function, however, allows any training programme they develop to be directly relevant and focused on the needs of their staff groups, but the issues of accreditation and the potential transferability of any course qualification are still unsolved.

Continuing staff development

So far we have been concentrating our discussion on the needs of basic-grade staff and in particular the induction requirements of those newly recruited to work in secure units. The same issues apply, however, to on-going training and career development. As we have indicated, within the prison service there is a notional trail to follow for gaining promotions and an accompanying series of training programmes to support that progression. This is less so in local authority secure units where although internal promotion is the most common way to fill vacancies there is no accompanying structured training programme apart from whatever an individual unit may create. Career advancement outside of the unit, whether in social work or an allied field, almost always brings with it the requirement for a Diploma in Social Work qualification and the associated difficulties of accessing the necessary training course. The situation is even more dire when considering the needs of those taking up management posts in secure units. Although there may be some degree of management training within the prison service structure, the content of this is not related to the management of units looking after young people or to the kinds of issues identified earlier in Chapter 7. Outside the prison service there is even less provision for management training and hardly anything for residential managers, let alone those who work in secure units. The feedback from managers at the Sheffield 2000 Conference revealed that no one had received any specific training for management in a secure environment and that only a few had received any general management training likely to be of relevance to them in their chosen area of work. That this situation exists is a serious indictment of the way in which this area of professional work has been regarded over the years and of the continuing low status ascribed to residential care.

Of particular concern is the absence of a coherent programme of training and support for managers who take on the responsibility of being Senior Manager in a secure unit. As well as dealing with the pressures of such an appointment there are whole areas of the management task which most people will not have much direct experience of before taking up post. Financial management plays an increasing part in the workload of Senior Managers, as does strategic planning across the whole range of functions. Making provision for this important group of managers must be considered a priority.

It is to the credit of the Youth Justice Board that, amongst all the competing demands on resources that it has faced, training has been prioritised to the extent that it has. In determining to create a coherent system of youth justice services with common levels of service and standards across England and Wales, the Board has had to confront the dual task of making an immediate impact on current services, which are characterised by disparate organisational arrangements and patchy delivery, whilst at the same time planning for the long-term development of integrated community interventions and secure provision. To this end there have been a number of training initiatives, including an initial training package for new staff in both secure units and Youth Offending Teams to participate in together. All of these have been delivered amidst doubts about the logistical possibility of bringing together large numbers of residentially based staff from the different types of secure unit and also of including staff from Youth Offending Teams. Some of these difficulties arise from the very tight time scales within which much of this training has been organised to date, and also from the inevitable reluctance of the service providers to get fully on board with a training programme in which they have not yet developed complete confidence.

It is a huge task to bring together all youth justice agencies, including secure units, into a coherent system to which staff feel allegiance and commitment and within which they see a range of career opportunities. An important part of this co-ordinating and development work has been done in partnership with relevant National Training Organisations (NTOs). An initial exercise was commissioned which attempted to scope areas of work which need to be covered in developing a set of occupational standards relevant to the professional needs of staff working in the youth justice field. From this preliminary study it is clear that although drawing upon existing standards in related areas of work covers certain aspects, there are a number of areas in which new standards will have to be developed in order to address the particular and specific needs of staff working with this client group, whether in secure accommodation or in the community. One of the main considerations in developing pathways towards the gaining of relevant awards in youth justice has to be the current range of professional backgrounds of staff in post. Some staff may want an award in this area to supplement and advance their previous professional qualifying training, especially if in the longer term they are intending to return to that area of work. The majority of staff, however, particularly those working in secure units, require training to a qualifying level. This model obviously can accommodate these varying levels of need, but this does not simplify the logistical difficulties associated with delivering highly differentiated training programmes or undertaking demanding NVQ assessments.

A model of training for residential staff in secure units

Even from our cursory look at the way in which social work training has developed over the years it is clear that working with children and young people in residential settings has never been a priority in terms of an emerging or wider curriculum. In fact there has never been a satisfactory resolution to the question as to whether or not residential work is in fact part of the wider social work function or a distinct discipline that should rightly have its own professional status and training. In my view it is clear from experience that residential work with children and young people, both in open and secure settings, is a discrete area of professional work and as such requires a separate structure for the training and development of its workforce. This may be linked to broader social work training but the specific demands that are made on staff who work in these environments indicate that unless the setting is understood and the core residential tasks are placed at the centre of the training experience then workers will not be properly prepared. In similar vein if the training experience does not take into account the way in which the residential task impinges upon both young people and adult workers then it will inevitably sell staff short as they encounter these realities for themselves. The same principles apply to management training and the needs of staff who move into management posts as part of their career progression. Managing a residential facility brings a unique set of challenges and requires a knowledge and skill base that is specific to the setting. This is even more the case where the unit is secure and placement involves the loss of liberty for children and young people.

It is commendable that the Youth Justice Board in establishing a model for staff development and training has recognised the specific requirements of staff working in the youth justice field as a discrete area of professional practice and has included in that those staff working in secure units. This represents a considerable advance for residential work as an area of professional work and should be embraced as such. Of course it leaves open the question about general residential services for young people and the training of staff for these settings, but current developments should enable a dovetailing of accreditation in both areas, and staff gaining awards through their work in secure accommodation may then transfer to other residential posts using that accreditation and vice versa.

The problem of retaining staff

All organisations in planning for the development of their staff face the tension between providing immediate and direct training to equip individuals for the tasks that in their current post they are expected to perform, and providing them with sufficient opportunities to develop their skills for the furtherance of their career. For larger organisations the latter is a worthwhile investment, particularly if there is a diversity of work settings and positions into which staff can move on a planned progression. Increasingly, however, for all professionals on whatever career path including social care, there is a decreasing likelihood of remaining in one organisation for the length of a working life. With greater mobility, people need to be able to undertake accredited training that has credibility from employer to employer, to develop their own career plans and to create their own opportunities for career advancement. Within secure units long-standing problems of staff recruitment have resulted in managers focusing their resources on the immediate training needs of staff, and on trying to retain their best staff through a process of internal promotion rather than encouraging their participation in broader, professional training. The result of this is to increase the number of staff who on being thwarted in advancing their career in a particular secure unit move into another area of work, and so the initial training investment is lost to residential services as a whole. The greater co-ordination of youth justice services and the planned development of an integrated accreditation system to allow staff to move across the boundaries not just of the different sectors of the secure estate but into community posts as well within Youth Offending Teams will greatly increase career development opportunities for residential workers. A proviso to this must be the need to guard against an exodus of residential staff into community-based posts. The real challenge is to reverse this trend by making the work of secure units an attractive, stimulating alternative, and, as Rose and Staniscia (1989) point out, this has much to do with the way in which managers in secure units create the environment for both the staff and young people.

Developing a curriculum

A good deal of the above depends on the success of the Youth Justice Board in establishing a more unified youth justice system and engaging the large number of different agencies involved in the development of a co-ordinated approach to the training of their respective staff resources. This is an enormous and complex organisational task to which at the same time there is a political dimension, as central government support to the pursuit of the ideal is a continuing requirement. Given, however, that this is the way things appear to be shaping, and that on the whole these are positive moves for the development of secure accommodation, what are the dangers and pitfalls? A significant one has already begun to emerge in the early work undertaken both within the original scoping exercise and in the identification of specific areas of work for which occupational standards are to be developed. A further difficulty is that there is no real research-based evidence to show in what ways training does improve staff performance in residential care settings or to what extent it makes a significant difference in the outcomes for young people (Sinclair and Gibbs 1996). Although it is reasonable to assume that a trained workforce is more effective than an untrained one, the questions remain as to what the content of that training should be and in what ways it should be delivered. Both of these issues reinforce the critical importance of properly defining the residential task and of having a clear and robust model which encapsulates the purpose of secure units and the complex dynamics that impinge upon the work of all staff both within and externally.

What is clear from experience is that unless the core tasks of the residential routine are acknowledged as fundamental areas in which staff must acquire professional expertise then they will continue to be exposed to situations for which they have received little by way of preparation, about which they have little knowledge and yet which occasion them massive anxiety on a day-to-day basis. To support this learning, staff must be given a thorough grounding in all aspects of child and adolescent development and an understanding of the importance of pro-social role modelling, with some opportunities to practise the skills in a residential setting. Without this core experience the ability of staff to tolerate and manage the 'in your face' behaviour which the young people exhibit on an almost minute-by-minute basis in the units will be seriously limited. At the same time young people will continue to be placed in secure residential settings where they are expected to engage in educational activities and offending behaviour programmes, but at the same time the context for those activities, i.e. the living group, is poorly organised and its influence potentially damaging to any of the work that might otherwise be productively undertaken. In other words staff need training not just in delivering the formal activities of a regime but in the management of the day-to-day residential routines within which these activities are set and which in themselves have considerable impact on young people.

It is in the development of a sound knowledge base for this work and the identification of the range of skills required that the real challenge lies for the creation of appropriate training programmes. The same mistakes that have dogged the development of training for residential workers over the years must not be allowed to prevail at a time when there are real opportunities to redefine the model of practice in secure accommodation with young people. What follows is an earlier attempt to sketch out a model for a training programme for staff working in conditions of security:

Knowledge Base
- Legal grounds for deprivation of liberty
- The rights of young people in security
- The need for planning with clear aims and objectives in case-work
- Understanding of the juvenile justice system and its management as part of the process in working with young offenders
- Understanding of the impact of 'systems' on young people and the nature of institutional abuse
- Understanding of child and adolescent development and the consequences of disturbance on the process

Skill Development
- Delivering primary care in a secure environment, for example, how to use routines in a way that maximises individual choice in a setting that emphasises group control; the importance of food and meal times in the care process; making the times of waking up and going to bed important and potentially therapeutic rather than institutional rituals accompanied by the jangling of keys

- Ensuring privacy whilst maintaining secure boundaries, for example welcoming and supervising visitors; protecting young people and staff by making certain that the unit is free of dangerous objects
- Managing difficult behaviour by emphasising other ways of conflict resolution other than physical strength; involving young people in decisions; giving regular and consistent feedback on behaviour and genuinely listening to what young people have to say
- The planning and delivery of imaginative activities
- The development of assessment, observational and recording techniques

Values
- The skills and knowledge required of staff in a secure unit have to be built on a value system where the needs of the young people are paramount and their interests are clearly defined. These values must include trust in young people, regard for rights above notions of treatment and due regard to issues of race and gender.

(J. Rose 1991)

Although it is over ten years since the above article was written, the issues remain pertinent and the same themes still need to be addressed when trying to define a curriculum for residential staff working in secure units.

In the same way that staff working directly with young people need access to a comprehensive training programme leading to some form of accredited award, so too do managers in secure units. The specific demands of work with young people in secure conditions have to be identified and the specific skills and knowledge required to manage these need to be incorporated into future models of training or pathways to accreditation for managers at all levels. First line, middle and senior managers may have different responsibilities according to their role within the organisation and require specific support in developing the relevant skills they need to fulfil them, but the setting in which they manage brings common issues and problems with which they each have to contend. The same applies to Governors, Directors and Centre Managers of secure units. The transition from managing as part of a team of peers to taking overall charge of an establishment looking after young people makes considerable demands on the individuals involved. This is not just at the level of acquiring additional skills, such as strategic planning, but in the assuming of the sole responsibility for an establishment and its staff teams and developing the necessary qualities of leadership which these posts require.

More than training

The task of making the training available for all staff in secure units, including managers, relevant to the core tasks of each staff group, as well as systematic and accessible in terms of its delivery, is clearly an urgent and important priority. However, training on its own is not enough to sustain the work of staff and to provide the ongoing support that they need to engage effectively and fully in their day-to-day work. For training to be effective it has to be delivered within the context of a wider culture in which the development of staff, at all levels and in all posts, is a real and planned part of the strategic approach an organisation takes to its work. At the macro level this requires each sector of the secure estate – prison service, local authority secure units, and secure training centres – to be committed with the Youth Justice Board to planning and delivering a comprehensive programme for staff training, in which the prescribed standards for delivery of services incorporate the regular occurrence of team meetings, handovers and professional supervision of all staff. At a micro level it means that managers must recognise the importance of staff development and be committed to ensuring that this remains a priority even when there seem to be competing and overwhelming demands to do something else.

We have identified the building blocks for the support of staff, which include training, supervision, team meetings and handovers, but in addition to these it is worth remembering the impetus for the development of staff that comes from role modelling by experienced colleagues. This can be a highly effective means of staff support, not just in the informal situations that arise in the course of the daily routines but also in more formal settings such as case reviews. Almost any situation brings opportunities for learning and it is important that staff take the time to talk to each other and reflect on such matters as what happened in a case review meeting or why someone visiting the unit reacted in an unexpected way. These sorts of conversation should be a regular feature of life within a secure unit and play a part in creating and maintaining an enquiring and supportive environment in which staff are encouraged to grow and develop. We have already identified the dangers that may overtake staff and the unit as a whole if these structures are not provided and sustained. It is not too strong a way of putting it to say that effective staff support is a matter of survival, certainly for individual staff, but in another way for young people as well. The underlying purpose of a support structure is not just the professional development of staff but the psychological containment of the young people in the unit, and if this is not provided then we have seen how chaos follows. A culture in which thinking is highly regarded and opportunities for staff to reflect and talk about what is going on are protected is a culture in which young people are much more likely to feel safe and looked after, and in which their personal and individual needs are adequately met.

Developing and using appropriate resources

So far we have considered the issues of staff support and development from a management perspective expressed in terms of their responsibility for ensuring that the unit is organised in a way that provides for the consistent delivery of routines for staff and young people. There is a further issue which is about the availability of professional expertise to support that delivery and how scarce resources are best allocated to provide maximum benefit. Staff already working in the secure estate have a great deal of experience and expertise which should be much better utilised to provide training for staff across all sectors. Senior staff within units have a wealth of experience and knowledge and, if the time were made available, could offer much to less experienced colleagues through the various models of formal supervision. Making better use of current resources is something that every organisation needs to constantly review, especially as employing external consultants for staff support and training at both the macro and micro levels is an expensive option. It also carries the risk that unless the consultants are well briefed and ideally have a real sense of how secure units function, they may not attract the credibility that professionals in the field demand of their trainers. In most secure units, outside of the line management structure, the disciplines of psychology and psychiatry tend to have the most important roles in supporting staff and contributing to the development of the culture as a whole. In particular it is the specialisms of child and adolescent forensic work that are of most value for secure units.

We have previously described the difficulties of recruiting suitably qualified personnel in this field and the variable level of provision of these services across the country. Despite this national shortage there are some very good examples of secure units which have either entered into a contractual arrangement with a health authority for the delivery of these services or which have established independent contracts with individual consultants on a sessional basis. These examples provide an interesting range of models of how these specialist resources and services may be utilised to provide quality assessments for young people in placement and at the same time offer a supportive and educational service for the benefit of residential staff. Such arrangements are not necessarily without their difficulty as there are issues of professional boundaries and clinical management to be resolved.

Confidentiality is a key issue for residential settings where a number of professionals from different disciplines might be involved with an individual young person. Residential staff often feel isolated if they are not regarded as equal professionals in the overall case management and treatment processes, and if they are excluded then any opportunities for a young person to 'split' the professionals involved with them are greatly increased. In the end the responsibility for all aspects of the management and care of a young person placed in a secure unit has to rest with the Senior Manager of that establishment. It is their responsibility throughout the organisation to create the structures for inter-disciplinary meetings and forums for discussion of casework and treatment issues to do with the young people in the unit. It is then the responsibility of the various professional groups to share with their colleagues the nature and content of their work so that a holistic view may be obtained about the ongoing needs and progress of each young person.

Allied to these difficulties is the perennial problem in these situations as to the proportion of time to be spent in individual or occasional group work with young people, and the proportion of time to be allocated for supervision and support of staff, which may also include both individual or group work. The Senior Manager of the unit again faces competing demands in deciding how these resources are best used. External agencies such as the Youth Offending Team responsible for a young person often see the time spent in a secure unit as an opportunity for assessments to be updated and to seek a specialist opinion which otherwise might not be available to them. Their request for an 'assessment' may well conflict with the view of staff in the unit whose day-to-day concerns about the safe management of a young person lead them to soak up the 'experts'' time as a way of meeting their own, very real needs.

The ways in which these issues are resolved and the kind of balance that is achieved between the two tasks are indicative of the extent to which a unit has taken on board the importance of providing support to its teams of residential staff and its recognition of the central and critical importance of their work to the overall organisational objectives. There is no doubt that individual clinical work is important and necessary –

indeed such work can of itself provide excellent role-modelling opportunities for residential staff to observe good practice from which they can learn. However, if time is scarce, as is most likely to be the case, then priority should be given to the role of psychologists and psychiatrists in supporting the residential staff, through some form of either group or individual supervision, and hence in supporting the culture through influencing the work of its chief carriers.

Summary

The journey from chaos to culture which we have sought to map in the specific context of work in secure units with young people may be seen as occurring at individual, group, organisational and even societal levels. For young people to embark on this journey through the experience of being placed in a secure unit means that the unit must be a place in which their anxieties can be safely contained and their antisocial behaviours managed and challenged in a way that creates opportunities for them to begin thinking about what needs to happen in order for things to change. Staff working in secure units need a model of practice which provides both a set of ideas that helps them to understand the complex relationships in which they are enmeshed as a result of their day-to-day work, and a range of identifiable skills which they must develop in order to engage effectively with young people. The psychological containment that both staff and young people require to undertake their respective and joint tasks successfully, and so fulfil the business of the secure unit, requires intelligent and skilled management. Managers of secure units must not only understand the importance of, but also have the will and commitment to provide, a framework of organisational and clinical support that consistently meets the needs of their staff groups on a continuing basis. The secure unit as a whole must be boundaried by a strong and integrated management system in which internal and external managers work closely together to contain the extreme anxieties which these institutions generate. It is only by bringing these components together that a model begins to take shape in which the practice and management of secure units can be located and in which the impossible may become just slightly easier.

Chapter 9

The extraordinary ordinary

The old saying, 'the devil is in the detail', applies in a particularly relevant way to residential work. However important the big picture may be, for a young person in a secure unit what matters is the single events, incidents and relationships that make up the day-to-day world that they inhabit. Beyond that world there are families, friends and communities about whom they think and to whom, at some point, they are most likely to return. Adults who work as members of staff in a secure unit are also mainly concerned with the routine events of their daily business and with keeping their performance of these duties fresh and enthusiastic. They have the additional responsibility, however, of looking beyond these activities and, through reflection and talking, making connections between what is going on in the present and what has gone before. A further task arises from this: to engage with young people in ways that encourage them to share in that reflective activity, to begin to make connections for themselves and to learn from the experience about how things might change in the future. It is precisely this process of thinking about the links between past and present, learning about how things might be done differently and trying to move on in a new way that encapsulates the fundamental purpose of secure units for the young people who are placed in them.

Regimes

We have continually emphasised the significance of the overall environment in a secure unit for achieving positive outcomes for young people, but within this a number of important activities must happen in as co-ordinated and integrated a manner as possible. As well as stimulating young people to think about their lives, placement in a secure unit offers opportunities to acquire a range of skills which should equip them for release into the community and reduce the likelihood of further offending.

The constituent parts of a regime for this group of young people therefore must include: a purposeful, relevant education programme which is continuous with external provision and offers similar accreditation; offending behaviour programmes which address the assessed needs of the young people and are compliant with the principles of the body of knowledge emerging from the 'What Works' research; a high level of health care provision that not only provides all necessary treatment but encourages young people to review their lifestyle and consider more healthy options for the future. This review should include substance-related issues and sexual health. In addition the mental health needs of each young person should be a priority whilst in custody, seeking to ensure that the experience of being locked up does not exacerbate underlying problems and that any serious mental illness is properly diagnosed and treated. Finally, contact with families and any other significant figures should be maintained and supported in as positive a way as possible through casework meetings, visits and other opportunities that may exist.

Maintaining a focus on longer-term objectives and planning for the future are often pushed to the bottom of the agenda, particularly if the young person is presenting severe management difficulties in the unit. As in most situations, resources and attention tend to get directed towards the most pressing problems and other issues become neglected. In order to minimise this happening it is essential that the casework planning processes centre on a young person's links with their family and others from a young person's home community such as Youth Offending Team workers, teachers, youth workers or Connexion workers. The involvement of families is of vital importance if any of the learning that may occur in the unit is to be transferred and built upon when a young person returns home.

Achieving an integrated approach

One of the main challenges for secure units is to integrate the different strands of their regime into a coherent programme for each young person, so that their individual needs are accommodated but at the same time they also benefit from the experience of group life through the course of routine daily activities. The 'What Works' research indicates that interventions which are targeted on the assessed and identifiable needs of each young person are more likely to be effective than those which simply take a 'scatter gun' approach and spray young people with an uncoordinated range of disparate activities, however worthwhile or interesting these may appear. However, the daily routines of group living are precisely the activities that form the core of a young person's experience during their period in custody and, as we have argued throughout this book, the relationships that they establish with staff and other young people, primarily through shared participation in ordinary daily life, are a shaping factor in how they respond to other elements of the regime. The here and now occurrences of daily life are the main focus of young people's interest and energy whilst they are in secure accommodation. Often these routines and structures provide a welcome relief from the stresses and strains which they have been experiencing in life outside, and in finding a certain amount of relief from these some young people become almost over-compliant and passive in their response to the regime. With these young people the task is to try to actively motivate them to make the best of their time in secure accommodation and gently encourage them into taking responsibility and moving on. For other young people their resistance to the approaches of staff is likely to be more aggressive or hostile, and in these instances staff have to initially manage whatever behaviour is exhibited and then try to work with the young person to develop more positive attitudes. In both cases the locus within which this work of engaging a young person takes place is the routine daily activities of residential life. This is not a process that can have any formal setting or structured approach. There are motivational programmes for young people which provide staff with material to use in their efforts to help a young person become involved in a programme, but in the end it is down to the way in which staff are able to understand the needs of a young person and relate these needs to experience in the unit.

The experience of a supportive and positive residential environment matters to young people in secure units, and the commonplace activities and exchanges which this comprises have enormous therapeutic power. The responsibility for creating this environment rests largely upon the shoulders of residential staff – the care workers or prison officers – who are the primary carers and role models for the young people. This is the meaning of the 'extraordinary ordinary' as a way of describing the potent effect of ordinary experiences and positive relationships with adults, which for most of the young people have not been part of their previous lifestyle or indeed played any significant part in their growing up.

Using ideas

In order to withstand the pressures that day-to-day contact with young people places upon residential and other staff who work in the secure environment, we have previously identified a tool box of ideas to which staff need access and from which they need to draw in order that they may be helped to understand the meaning of the behaviours with which they are confronted. By applying these ideas, a clearer understanding emerges, not only about what is happening in the present, but light is shed on each young person's particular story about their earlier life. In similar vein, staff must develop their knowledge of the context within which they are working, including the role of secure units and other agencies in the youth justice system. This means becoming more aware of the wider expectations that society has about the purpose of secure units and the professionals who work with young offenders. In the same way that staff want to find out about young people's stories, they also need to know something about the ways in which social policies have shaped services and provision for delinquent and disturbed young people, how these have changed over the years and what factors have affected public attitudes in this area. Another part of the knowledge base for staff comes from studying different traditions of residential child care and incorporating the lessons that can be learned from these into models of practice which may then be applied to their work in secure units.

Developing skills

As well as developing their capacity to think, staff must also develop the broad range of skills which are necessary to engage young people in the diverse programme of activities which make up the regime in a secure unit. For the most part these skills are exercised in the course of working with young people through the ordinary events of daily life, although there are occasions when residential staff are involved in the more formal and specific elements of education or offending behaviour programmes. To form relationships with young people that are at one and the same time purposeful and supportive, staff must develop a high degree of personal maturity and self-awareness. The individual qualities that each member of staff possesses feed into and enhance the repertoire of skills that are needed to manage the challenging behaviour which young people present to them. Humour, perseverance, tolerance and emotional strength are also necessary because, as we have seen, attacks from young people are not just physical but are directed at the most sensitive and core elements of each member of staff's character, appearance or personality. All of the above are building blocks for the role that staff play as significant adults or pro-social role models in and through their relationships with young people as they work with them on a daily basis.

It is interesting to see how the processes that underpin work in secure units are essentially the same for both staff and young people, and consist of thinking, talking and acquiring skills to cope more positively with situations and other people. For staff the focus of their work is on how these may be used for the benefit of each young person in the unit for whom they have responsibility, as well as on their own professional and personal development. Many of the young people in a secure unit are too damaged to do much of this work for themselves, although the possibilities for each must be explored and taken to their full potential.

Making connections

An important aspect of the thinking which staff at all levels in a secure unit have to do is to make connections between events or comments that may at first sight seem unrelated or to have nothing in common. The basis of this is experience which indicates that in a secure unit everything is connected and that only by taking a holistic approach to understanding what is going on can the total picture emerge. This is why establishing forums for staff from different disciplines to meet and share information is critical, as are the systems which should be in place to collate and monitor all incidents or other received intelligence. It is also important for each young person to know that they are being contained in a way that holds all parts of their life together and that the adults who are looking after them know about what matters. Of course, there may be some resistance to this as young people act defensively to avoid that kind of wholeness being created. Having to confront their previous experience may be so anxiety-provoking for a young person that they will seek to preserve their safety by 'splitting' the adults around them rather than having everything known.

Connecting the past with the present and the internal with the external are continuous activities for secure units and have application and relevance at individual, organisational and societal levels. Each young person has their own personal history which enshrines the events through which they have passed and which has brought them to their present situation and placement in a secure unit. Along the way they have developed their own unique internal world which seeks to understand and make sense of what has happened or is happening. Often, because of the nature of their experience, these understandings are distorted and lead a young person to behave in the external world in ways that are highly antisocial, delinquent and dangerous. The overall therapeutic task has to be to help them to connect these experiences, understand them and try to think differently about how they might behave in response. The role of staff in a secure unit may only be to support a part of that process through the nature of the experience that a young person has whilst placed in the unit, but it is an essential stage of the long trail that each young person is following. A complicating factor for this is that work in secure units is not solely with individuals but has a strong group element which may subsume the individual and at the very least influences the way they behave and react. For staff, therefore, their thinking has to take into account not only each individual's past and present circumstances, their internal thoughts and external behaviours, but also those of the group as well.

Organisations as well as individuals have a past, and traditions and history influence present organisational life in ways that are not always immediately apparent. Contributing powerfully to this are the informal stories which are repeatedly told and which maintain what may become fixed views about what a particular secure unit is like to work in or as a placement for young people. Organisations have to balance their internal pressures and stresses with those that come from the world beyond their walls. The high levels of anxiety and fantasy which attach to secure units can be a significant factor in shaping what goes on inside and influence in almost imperceptible ways staff behaviour and attitudes.

In similar ways at a wider, societal level the influence of history in the way social policies have changed with regard to the care of delinquent young people is evident in the current design of provision of secure accommodation for young people, and there is also an internal world of anxiety and fantasy which fuels the way public attitudes are shaped with regard to delinquency and young offenders.

The model in Figure 9.1 seeks to illustrate the complex relationships which are outlined above.

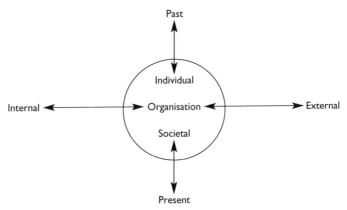

Figure 9.1

The summary outline above of the main themes of *Working with Young People in Secure Accommodation* demonstrates the complexity of the task that faces secure units. Central to achieving any success is the presence of a strong management culture that is able to provide both leadership and structure for the various staff groups. Allied to this must be a coherent and responsive system for the support, supervision and training of those groups of staff, which is founded on a real knowledge and understanding about the developmental needs of young people and the practical needs of staff who work with them in a secure environment.

The secure estate – strengths and weaknesses

There are currently three providers of secure accommodation for young people in England and Wales: the prison service, local authorities and independent companies who own and manage secure training centres. Each of these have their respective strengths and weaknesses and make a distinctive contribution to the care and treatment of delinquent, disturbed young people. Although their organisational and management arrangements vary, the issues that each type of secure accommodation faces with regard to the care of young people are very similar and this is especially true in those matters that affect staff and managers in their daily work. In order to try to develop a model of theory and practice for looking after young people in secure conditions it is necessary to review current provision and attempt at least a partial analysis of what each provider has to offer and the opportunities and problems that they face in the future. We have already pointed out the historical pathways that secure units have trodden in order to reach their present position, and the lack of connection that has existed between them. The separation of the ways in which penal and child care residential services have developed has not been at all to the benefit of young people, who have moved between establishments and through different systems with little or no co-ordinated planning. Different professional groups with very different values and intentions have disjointedly tried to provide for exactly the same groups of children and young people. The Youth Justice Board represents an opportunity to address this lack of connection, provided that it keeps itself open to consider the wider needs of children and young people in relation to the use of secure accommodation and other forms of welfare provision.

Young Offender Institutions

The prison service is currently the largest provider of secure accommodation for young people between 15 and 18 years of age. We have described the changes in the way this group is looked after, the separation of facilities and the prescription of regime standards tailored towards addressing the special difficulties they face. The prison service has a long history of managing troubled people whose behaviour has exhausted other attempts to care for them. This has been no less true with young people, and Young Offender Institutions have plenty of examples to share about young people placed in them who could not be managed in any alternative setting. There is also a strong tradition in prison service establishments of vocational training, and many units have well-resourced workshop facilities and these present opportunities which make a particular appeal to young people disaffected with more formal approaches to their education. The prison service has a strong management structure and stability of staffing which is of importance in managing difficult people. The overall size of the organisation and the availability of resources also make the prison service able to provide a large number of placements at a relatively low cost per place.

On the other hand it is the size of most Young Offender Institutions which militates against providing the kind of individual and personalised care programmes which, as we have seen, are essential for meeting the needs of a very young, vulnerable and damaged group of people. Although staffing is stable, in prison service establishments the ratios between staff and young people are very low, which makes it almost impossible to pay sufficient attention to the needs of each young person or to relate to a living group in a close enough way to significantly impact on their attitudes and behaviour. Residential accommodation, with some notable exceptions, is poor and cannot provide for the necessary high level of personal care which these young people need. Training has not yet been focused enough on supporting staff in their work with a younger adolescent group or identifying the core body of skills needed to engage with them. Achieving the shift in culture required to make under-18 prison service establishments young-person-centred has still got a very long way to go.

However, the prison service has shown that it has the will to be involved in the care of this age group in secure accommodation, and realistically in the foreseeable future it is going to be a major player in this field. The numbers of young people placed with the prison service will almost certainly reduce as alternative forms of accommodation come on stream. Having a large and flexible capacity to provide placements, in an environment where the numbers of young people sentenced to custody are at best variable and at worst may increase, is a strong suit to have in your hand. The argument as to whether or not any young people should be placed in prison-service-managed establishments will no doubt continue. Ideally it might be better for a complete separation of the under-18 estate to occur. Whilst this would allow for dedicated management and for staff to develop their distinctive identity, the organisational task of achieving this and attracting sufficient numbers of staff to transfer out of the prison service without jeopardising the rest of the service would be considerable. The challenge for the prison service is to maintain the progress that has been made in terms of the quality of care and programmes available to young people, but to embrace more emphatically the fact that the task of caring for young people really is qualitatively different and requires staff to develop special knowledge and skills.

Local authority secure units

Local authority secure units are low-volume, high-quality providers of secure accommodation. No unit in this sector has more than 40 places and most operate with between 16 and 24. A major refurbishment and building programme has been undertaken in this sector during the past ten years, which has resulted in the achievement of an overall very high standard of accommodation and facilities in most of the units. High staffing ratios, specialist education facilities and access to external resources combine to make it more possible for young people to receive individual care and attention which can then be targeted and focused on their specific needs and problems. In particular, personal care is provided to a very high order and social and leisure activities offer wide-ranging opportunities. The attention to detail which can be given to a young person's programme and the level of individual work which they can receive in all areas result in often quite dramatic progress being made. The smaller size of these units makes them particularly well-equipped to deal with more complex problems which a young person may have, especially where close supervision is required and a number of agencies are involved in the case planning. The ability of the units to provide individual care programmes also makes them a more suitable resource for young women than a larger prison service unit. A number of the units are mixed-gender and at least two offer placements for young women alone. For staff as well, supervision and training are recognised as important and there are opportunities for access to departmental training programmes as part of the secure unit's role within social services.

However, a number of the positive factors identified above also serve as disadvantages. Low size has tended to equate to high cost and although this is partly explained in terms of facilities and staffing levels there are a number of questions that remain to be answered about value for money and economy of scale. The individual management of these units by separate local authorities also means differences in service levels and standards. Although every unit is inspected by the national Social Services Inspectorate against common standards, the very local nature of their resourcing and management does result in varying levels of practice and certainly in widely differing levels of external support and involvement from other agencies. It also means that staff in the units are working in relative isolation from other professionals in the secure accommodation field, with only limited opportunities for inter-professional liaison. Although the units are able to provide for individual needs and look after some very troubled young people, the resources for managing the most extreme acting out behaviours can be exhausted quite quickly. This is particularly so if there is a child protection dimension, as separation of young people into different groupings is not always possible, given limited space. Tensions may exist in these units between the needs of young people sentenced by the court and the needs of those who are placed for their own protection on welfare orders. Managing this mix adds to the complexity of an already difficult series of tasks. Although as we identified in Chapter 7 staffing ratios are high, the level of training and qualification amongst staff groups is variable.

In the context of the Youth Justice Board and the creation of a secure estate the role of local authority secure units has come under particular scrutiny. Cost differentials inevitably come into the picture, with a placement in a local authority secure unit being at least four times the cost of an average prison service placement. The reasons for this may seem apparent but with these go accompanying expectations about quality of service and the capacity to manage the most difficult of young people. The dilemma of whether or not the units serve a justice or a welfare population has been ongoing for a long time, certainly pre-Youth Justice Board. The arrival of the Board has, however, served to sharpen the focus of the debate. Local authority secure units are an important part of the national provision of secure accommodation, as their size and ethos are undoubtedly beneficial for meeting the needs of disturbed and needy young people. In fact it is this ethos and its underpinning values about young people that has provided the model for developments in the prison service. For the future it will become even more important that local authority secure units should be able to define more cogently their specific role within the wider system of secure units and become more explicit about what it is they offer and for whom they can best provide a service. A generic 'we take all comers' approach is likely to be undermined by an increase in the number of places provided by the independent sector and the continuing involvement of the prison service.

Secure training centres

Secure training centres are the most recent development in secure accommodation for young people and the first secure units provided by independent companies outside the public sector. Their initial arrival on the scene was greeted with a wave of opposition and scepticism about the ability of this sector to provide adequate standards of care, and also whether or not it could be morally justified to provide secure accommodation for young people on a profit basis. Undoubtedly the early days of the first of these centres at Medway in Kent were surrounded by controversy and high levels of public interest (Social Services Inspectorate 1999). Despite this somewhat fraught beginning there are now three secure training centres, and a planned programme of expansion by the Youth Justice Board would appear to make them the preferred means of providing custodial care for this age group. With an operational capacity of around forty places, although expansion and newer designs will increase this to nearer eighty, secure training centres combine the security features of prison service establishments with the standards of residential accommodation and staffing approaches of local authority secure units. They have been developed, however, for a single target group of young people aged between 12 and 15 years sentenced under, initially, the Secure Training Order and, more recently, the Detention and Training Order. This single focus has meant that regimes and programmes have been designed in such a way that a balance can be struck between the delivery of offending behaviour programmes and high levels of education, with the creation of an environment in which primary care and behaviour management are young-person-centred. The focus of the managing organisation, although the centres are part of larger company portfolios, is concentrated on the needs of each centre with no competing demands for the time and attention of its senior managers. The secure training centres have to operate in compliance with a tightly drawn up contract managed by the Youth Justice Board, which specifies a number of key inputs and outputs that have to be achieved and which are monitored on an ongoing basis.

Although the secure training centres have many advantages over both local authority and prison service provision they still experience the inevitable difficulties of the recruitment of qualified staff and then of retaining those in whom they invest heavily through in-house training courses. This has already begun to show as a problem as staff receiving good training opportunities in a secure training centre as well as valuable practical experience find that they can earn more money in another sector. A further challenge for the secure training centres will be in their development programme aimed at increasing the size of units and the numbers of young people placed on a single campus. In addition it is proposed that the age range of the young people admitted to the centres should formally be widened to include up to 18-year-olds, and that young people held on remand should also be admitted. As numbers grow and the role of the centres expands, maintaining an individual and young-person-focused approach as well as a strong care ethos may not be achieved unless staffing ratios, currently higher than the prison service but not as high as in local authority secure units, are kept at least at present levels. Without careful management there is clearly going to be a question of cost for these centres, which were always intended to be cheaper than local authority provision, if their high standards are to be developed still further.

We have considered elsewhere the key role of the Youth Justice Board not just in shaping the future of secure accommodation but for the whole of the youth justice system. The clearly stated purpose for the youth justice system, which echoes the political agenda and hence the expectations of the general public, is to prevent offending by young people. Whatever degree of scepticism such a broad aim might attract there can be no doubt arising from it as to where resources and energies are going to be put. The inherent dangers of ignoring the wide range of needs that young people, and especially those caught up in the criminal justice system, actually have should not be overlooked, and the challenge for all departments and agencies is to actually achieve the levels of closer working together to which central government policy aspires. These broader contexts cannot be ignored as we return to the central purpose of this book, to explore what kind of models of ideas and practice may be best employed for the design and operation of such highly sensitive and volatile organisations as secure units for young people.

Towards a model for secure units

The heart of *Working with Young People in Secure Accommodation* is the belief that within the overall environment of a secure unit the daily work of the core residential staff not only contributes to the delivery of the different elements of a regime but models its inherent values and thereby provides the ground for change to take place in the life of a young person. The relationships between staff and young people encapsulate a young person's experience in secure units and have value both for what they represent in their own right and as instruments for encouraging young people to engage in other aspects of the programme. To achieve this kind of environment staff must be well supported and managed and have available to them high levels of supervision and training.

The differences that exist between secure units include such things as their size, their management arrangements and their lines of accountability within the social welfare and justice systems. The historical development of different types of institution has often shaped their current roles and affects the way staff are recruited, trained and understand the nature of their work in a particular institution. The emergence of the Youth Justice Board has presented an opportunity to create a coherent secure estate for young people under the age of 18 years, and it has been made clear that there is a requirement for a single purpose and common standards to apply to all units whatever their organisational context.

The task, however, cannot be reduced to trying to create a uniform set of institutions operating under a single set of standards. Differences between the types of secure unit are potentially useful in meeting the wide and diverse needs of the young people who have to be accommodated. However, despite the obvious differences, what we have tried to show is that out of the common elements that exist between secure units it is possible to develop a coherent set of values that underpin work with young people and support the development of staff. The processes we have described that arise out of working in a secure environment with young people who have long and disturbing histories of antisocial and delinquent behaviour are the same for each secure unit. The significant effect that these processes have on individuals and whole staff groups occurs irrespective of setting. Understanding these processes and engaging with them in ways that promote a healthy and safe environment in which personal growth and change are stated objectives demand clear and informed management at all levels both within and outside the secure units themselves.

Throughout this book we have sought to explore the different parts of a possible model for secure accommodation for young people. This includes an external dimension, which must involve agreed policies about the role and function of secure units, as well as an internal organisation whose understanding of its purpose must be consistent with the externally stated aims and objectives. Internally as well, the organisation of a secure unit must be able to contain the high levels of anxiety that such environments generate, in order that staff are able to be focused on their work, which is to develop positive relationships with young people and behave as strong role models whilst delivering the necessary components of the regime.

In Chapter 3 we defined the ideal experience of a secure unit as offering to young people a 'corrective emotional experience'. This is a helpful way of thinking as it not only brings together the important cognitive work which must be attempted to challenge behaviour but places this in the context of a personal and emotional encounter with adults who may be relied upon to behave differently from those from earlier experiences. It is through these relationships and in the total context of a corrective emotional experience that the real challenges may be made to a young person's antisocial or offending behaviour and that a transition from chaos to culture becomes a reality for them. This is why any programme for evaluating the work of secure units, and indeed any consideration of an individual's progress during a period in secure accommodation, has to be able to assess the overall experience and not just focus on simple measures of input or output.

Irving Yalom, the distinguished American psychotherapist, is well known for his work with both individual patients and groups. In the following quotation he is writing about his work with an individual patient, but what he has to say has equal application to group work and also to our setting of a secure, residential unit. It bears witness to the prime significance of relationships and to the central importance of the work of residential staff and their relationships with young people during their time in a secure unit. These staff receive little by way of acknowledgement in terms of their daily work and yet their contribution is without doubt the most influential for what happens to a young person during their time in custody.

> When I first began to work as a therapist, I naively believed that the past was fixed and knowable; that if I was perspicacious enough, I could discover that false turn, that fateful trail that has led to a life gone wrong; and that I could act on this discovery and set things right again .... But over the years I have learned that the therapist's venture is not to join the patient in an archaeological dig. If any patients have ever been helped in that fashion, it wasn't because of the search and the finding of that false trail (a life never goes wrong because of a false trail; it goes wrong because the main trail is false). No, a therapist helps a patient not by sifting through the past but by being

lovingly present with that person; by being trustworthy, interested; and by believing that their joint activity will ultimately be redemptive and healing. The drama of age regression and incest recapitulation (or for that matter any therapeutic cathartic or intellectual project) is healing only because it provides therapist and patient with some interesting shared activity while the real therapeutic force – the relationship – is ripening on the tree. So I devoted myself to being present and faithful.

(Yalom 1989: 227)

Present and faithful: good words to describe the qualities for a residential worker in a secure unit.

References and suggestions for further reading

Ainsworth, F. (1978) 'Residential Work – A Strategy for Educational Development', unpublished paper, London: CCETSW.

Ashmore, Z. (2000) 'A Comparison of Two Secure Regimes for Male, Juvenile Offenders: Measuring Their Performance', unpublished M.St. Thesis, Institute of Criminology, University of Cambridge.

Audit Commission (1996) *Misspent Youth – Young People and Crime*, London: Audit Commission.

Bettelheim, B. (1950) *Love Is Not Enough*, New York: Glencoe Free Press.

Boswell, G. (1995) *Violent Victims. The Prevalence of Abuse and Loss in the Lives of Section 53 Offenders*, London: The Prince's Trust.

Bowlby, J. (1973) *Attachment and Loss*, Vol. II: *Separation, Anxiety and Anger*, London: Hogarth Press.

Bradfield, W. (1913) *The Life of Thomas Bowmer Stephenson*, London: Charles H. Kelly.

Brown, D. and Pedder, J. (1991) *Introduction to Psychotherapy*, London: Routledge.

Brown, E., Bullock, R., Hobson, C. and Little, M. (1998) *Making Residential Care Work: Structure and Culture in Children's Homes,* Aldershot: Ashgate Publishing.

Bullock, R., Little, M. and Millham, S. (1993) *Residential Care for Children: A Review of the Research*, London: HMSO.

Bullock, R., Little, M. and Millham, S. (1998) *Secure Treatment Outcomes*, Aldershot: Ashgate Publishing.

Burton, J. (1993) *The Handbook of Residential Care*, London: Routledge.

Cawson, P. and Martell, M. (1979) *Children Referred to Closed Units*, London: HMSO.

Cosgrave, N. (2000) 'Summary of Effective Practice', London: Orchard Lodge.

Cox, M. (1998) 'A Supervisor's View', in C. Cordess and M. Cox (eds) *Forensic Psychotherapy*, London and Philadelphia: Jessica Kingsley.

Crimmens, D. and Pitts, J. (2000) *Positive Residential Practice: Learning the Lessons of the 1990s*, Lyme Regis: Russell House Publishing.

Curtis Report (1946) 'Report of the Care of Children Committee', London: HMSO.

Davis, A. (1981) *The Residential Solution*, London: Tavistock.

Delshadian, S. (2001) 'Art Therapy with Disturbed Patients', *Prison Service Journal* 133.

Department of Health (annual publication) *Children Accommodated in Secure Units*, London: Government Statistical Service.

Ditchfield, J. and Catan, L. (1992) *Juveniles Sentenced for Serious Offences: A Comparison of Regimes in Young Offender Institutions and Local Authority Secure Homes*, London: Home Office.

Epps, K., Moore, C. and Hollin, C. (1999) 'Prevention and Management of Violence in a Secure Youth Centre', *British Journal of Therapy and Rehabilitation* 6 (2).

Erikson, E. (1965) *Childhood and Society*, Harmondsworth: Penguin.

Etzioni, A. (1961) *A Comparative Analysis of Complex Organisations*, New York: Glencoe Free Press.

Favazza, A. (1987) *Bodies under Siege*, Baltimore: Johns Hopkins University Press.

Fonagy, P. and Target, M. (1998) 'Personality and Sexual Development, Psychopathology and Offending', in C. Cordess and M. Cox (eds) *Forensic Psychotherapy,* London and Philadelphia: Jessica Kingsley.

Freud, A. (1946) *The Psycho-analytic Treatment of Children*, London: Imago.

Graham, J. and Bowling, B. (1995) *Young People and Crime*, London: HMSO.

Greenson, R.R. (1967) *The Technique and Practice of Psychoanalysis*, London: Hogarth Press.

Hagell, A., Hazel, N. and Shaw, C. (2000*) Evaluation of Medway Secure Training Centre*, London: Home Office.

Handy, C. (1978) *Gods of Management*, London: Souvenir Press.

Henggeler, S. (1999) 'Multisystemic Therapy: An Overview of Clinical Procedures, Outcomes and Policy Implications', *Child Psychology and Psychiatry Review* 4(1).

Hinshelwood, R.D. (1999) 'Psychoanalytic Origins and Today's Work: The Cassel Heritage', in P. Campling and R. Haigh (eds) *Therapeutic Communities: Past, Present and Future*, London: Jessica Kingsley.

HM Chief Inspector of Prisons (1997) *Young Prisoners: A Thematic Review*, London: Home Office.

HM Chief Inspector of Prisons (1999) *Suicide is Everyone's Concern: A Thematic Review*, London: Home Office.

HM Inspectorate of Prisons (1999) 'Treatment of Young People in Custody', London: HM Inspectorate of Prisons.

HM Prison Service (1999) 'Regimes for Prisoners under 18 Years Old: Prison Service Order 4950', London: HM Prison Service.

Hobbs and Hook Consulting (2000) 'Research into Effective Practice with Young People in Secure Facilities', London: Youth Justice Board.

Hollin, C. and Howells, K. (1996) *Clinical Approaches to Working with Young Offenders*, Chichester: Wiley.

Hollin, C., Epps, K. and Kendrick, D. (eds) (1995) *Managing Behavioural Treatment: Policy and Practice with Delinquent Adolescents*, London: Routledge.

Home Office (1991) 'The National Prison Survey', London: Home Office.

Home Office (1998) 'Youth Justice Task Force Report', London: Home Office.

Howe, D., Brandon, M., Hinings, D. and Schofield, G. (1999*) Attachment Theory, Child Maltreatment and Family Support*, London: Macmillan.

Hughes, L. and Pengelly, P. (1997) *Staff Supervision in a Turbulent Environment*, London: Jessica Kingsley.

Hutton, J., Bazalgette, J. and Armstrong, D. (1994) 'What Does Management Really Mean?', in R. Casemore (ed.) *What Makes Consultancy Work – Understanding the Dynamics*, London: Southbank University Press.

Kahan, B. (1994) *Growing Up in Groups*, London: HMSO.

Kerfoot, M. and Butler, A. (1988) *Problems of Childhood and Adolescence*, London: Macmillan.

Kets de Vries, M. (1980) *Organisational Paradoxes: Clinical Approaches to Management*, London: Tavistock.

Kurtz, Z., Thornes, R. and Bailey, S. (1998) 'Children in the Criminal Justice and Secure Care Systems: How their Mental Health Needs are Met', *Journal of Adolescence* 21: 543–553.

Lader, D., Singleton, N. and Meltzer, H. (1997) 'Psychiatric Morbidity among Young Offenders in England and Wales', London: Office for National Statistics.

Liebling, A., Elliot, C. and Price, D. (1999) 'Appreciative Inquiry and Relationships in Prison'*, Punishment and Society: The International Journal of Penology* 1(1): 71–98.

Likert. R. (1976) *New Ways of Managing Conflict*, Maidenhead: McGraw-Hill.

Lyon, J., Dennison, C. and Wilson, A. (2000) *'Tell Them So They Listen': Messages from Young People in Custody*, London: Home Office.

McGuire, J. (ed.) (1995) *What Works: Reducing Offending*, Chichester: Wiley.

Madge, N. (1994) *Children and Residential Care in Europe*, London: National Children's Bureau.

Menzies Lyth, I. (1959) 'The Functions of Social Systems as a Defence Against Anxiety: A Report on a Study of the Nursing Service of a General Hospital', *Human Relations* 13: 95–121.

Millham, S., Bullock, R. and Hosie, K. (1980) *Learning to Care: The Training of Staff for Residential Social Work with Young People*, Farnborough: Gower.

Mintzberg, H. (1973) *The Nature Of Managerial Work*, New York: Harper & Row.

Morgan, R. (1997) 'Imprisonment: Current Concerns And A Brief History since 1945', in M. Maguire, R. Morgan And R. Reiner (eds) *The Oxford Handbook Of Criminology*, Oxford: Clarendon.

O'Neill, T. (2001) *Children in Secure Accommodation*, London: Jessica Kingsley.

Pascale, R.T. and Athos, A.G. (1981) *The Art Of Japanese Management*, New York: Simon & Schuster.

Pitts, J. (1990) *Working with Young Offenders*, London: Macmillan.

Redl, F. (1966) *When We Deal With Children*, New York: The Free Press.

Redl, F. and Wineman, D. (1965) *Controls From Within*, New York: The Free Press.

Rose, J. (1991) 'A Pressing Need', *Community Care,* 22 August.

Rose, J. (1998) 'Tough Love Story', *Community Care,* 22–28 January.

Rose, J. and Staniscia, G. (1989) 'Training for Second Best?', *Insight,* 19 July.

Rose, M. (1990) *Healing Hurt Minds: The Peper Harow Experience*, London: Tavistock/Routledge.

Rutter, M. and Giller, H. (1983) *Juvenile Delinquency: Trends and Perspectives*, Harmondsworth: Penguin.

Rutter, M., Giller, H. and Hagell, A. (1998) *Antisocial Behaviour by Young People*, Cambridge: Cambridge University Press.

Sinclair, I. and Gibbs, I. (1996) *Quality of Care in Children's Homes*, Social Work Research and Development Unit, University Of York.

Sinclair, I. and Gibbs, I. (1998) *Children's Homes: A Study in Diversity*, Chichester: Wiley.

Social Exclusion Unit (1999) *Bridging the Gap: New Opportunities for 16–18 Year Olds Not in Education, Employment or Training*, London: The Stationery Office.

Social Services Inspectorate (1999) *Report of an Inspection of Medway Secure Training Centre*, London: Department of Health.

Utting, W. (1997) *People Like Us: The Report of the Review of Safeguards for Children Living Away from Home*, London: The Stationery Office.

Wheal, A. (1998) *Adolescence. Positive Approaches for Working with Young People*, Lyme Regis: Russell House Publishing.

Winnicott, D.W. (1956) 'The Antisocial Tendency', In D.W. Winnicott, *Collected Papers: Through Paediatrics to Psycho-analysis*, London: Tavistock.

Yalom, I. (1989) *Love's Executioner and Other Tales of Psychotherapy*, New York: Basic Books.

Yalom, I. (1998) *The Yalom Reader*, New York: Basic Books.

Young, R. (1995) 'Mental Space and Group Relations', paper presented at seminar on Group Relations and Organisational Behaviour, New Bulgarian University.

Youth Justice Board (2000) 'Review of the Year 1999–2000', London: Youth Justice Board.

Youth Justice Board (2001) Draft National Specification for Young People on a Detention and Training Order, London: Youth Justice Board.

Index